Naguib Mahfouz *at Sidi Gaber*

Reflections of a Nobel Laureate

1994–2001

From Conversations with Mohamed Salmawy

The American University in Cairo Press
Cairo New York

The American University in Cairo Press
113 Sharia Kasr el Aini, Cairo, Egypt
420 Fifth Avenue, New York, NY 10018
www.aucpress.com

Dar el Kutub No. 7146/01
ISBN 977 424 673 X

Designed by AUC Press Design Center/Andrea El-Akshar
Printed in Egypt

Contents

Introduction

In the early evening of Friday, 14 October 1994, the Arab world's leading man of letters Naguib Mahfouz was on his way to his weekly gathering with friends at one of the public cafés of Cairo. He stepped out of his house and had barely got into the car of one of his friends who had come to drive him to the meeting, when a young man thrust his hand through the car window.

Thinking that he was one of the innumerable fans who seek to shake hands with him, Mahfouz immediately stretched out his own hand, only to find that the young man's hand held a knife, which in a second was thrust into the old man's neck. Two very fortunate coincidences saved Mahfouz's life. First, the friend driving him was a physician, who immediately put his hand tightly on the wound, stopping the hemorrhage. Second, the incident happened almost in front of the Police Hospital, adjacent to Mahfouz's house, so that only a few minutes after the attempt on his life Mahfouz was in the operating room, surrounded by a fine team of surgeons.

At that time, the Egyptian police had cracked down very strongly on several fundamentalist groups who had carried out terrorist attacks in the name of Islam. In a desperate attempt to assert their waning power, these groups were seeking yet another resounding attack that would prove that they were still there and could still strike whenever they wanted. Mahfouz was an ideal choice as a target. A figure of world renown, his assassination would not pass unnoticed. It would assert not only to the Egyptian people but also to the whole world that fundamentalism had not been wiped out as the authorities had been claiming. And being weakened by successive crackdowns, these movements had to make sure that their target was not only a person with a world reputation, but that he was, first and foremost, easy to reach. Mahfouz had always refused all types of security guards, and he lived most of his life among the people in coffeeshops, where he would meet with friends, young literati, journalists, or simply anybody who wanted to talk with him. Furthermore, he has always been a great walker: he never had a car and liked to move on foot. Besides, almost all Cairo knew that every Friday evening, Mahfouz would leave his house at half past six for this weekly gathering that he had kept for years.

On the morning of 15 October, I was the first to see Mahfouz in his hospital room. Crowds of friends, men of letters, fans, and ordinary people, who had been horrified at the news of the attempt on the life of the man who in the national consciousness had become a symbol of Egypt itself, stood in shock in the hospital's courtyard all night waiting to hear how he was doing. When Mahfouz was told that I was outside, he immediately asked to see me. He greeted me with his usual jovial smile and asked me to thank the people who had flocked to the hospital and to tell them that he was all right.

And all right indeed he was, but not in his right arm, with the hand that had produced in over half a century more than forty novels, more than 350 short stories, and five short plays. The knife that had hit the right side of his neck had cut the nerve that runs through his right arm. We all thought Mahfouz's right arm was going to be paralyzed for life. But he was able, after he left the hospital, to carry out the doctors' instructions and exercise his right arm for half an hour every day. This, with the physiotherapy that he underwent three times a week, eventually resulted in his regaining the ability to hold the pen between his fingers. But his writing was no longer the large, clear letters that his friends knew so well. It looked more like the scribbling of a child's first attempts at writing. And, indeed, after having gained the world's greatest award for writing, Mahfouz was learning once again how to write at the age of 83.

This would have been enough to push anybody to despair. But not Mahfouz: he did it gladly day in, day out for months, for years, until he was able to write again, but never for more than half an hour a day. This precious half-hour he now keeps for his literary writings. Over the last few years he has been able to produce more than seventy shorts stories—very short ones, which take less than half an hour to write. The result has been little gems that, like Japanese haiku poetry, embodied in their excessive brevity the wisdom of life itself. These short stories are being published in the magazine *Nisf al-dunya* as *Dreams of Convalescence*.

As for his weekly column in Egypt's leading newspaper, *al-Ahram*, which he had written for almost twenty years, Mahfouz asked that it be turned into an interview, which I would conduct with him. It became more of a conversation, actually, where I would bring up a topic and wait to see what Mahfouz had to say about it. In publishing these conversations I would often omit my words altogether, leaving only the words of Mahfouz. I have suggested to Mahfouz that he publish his words as a column of his own, but he always refuses, saying that it is the conversation with me that brings about these thoughts and, as such, it should be presented to the reader as an interview. And so it has been. For close on seven years now, I have had the privilege and pleasure of conducting these conversations with Mahfouz every single week, and the resulting column has been appearing every Thursday in *al-Ahram* in Arabic and *Al-Ahram Weekly* in English. The present collection has been chosen from the English version.

At the suggestion of Mark Linz, the director of the American University in Cairo Press, I have collected in this book over one hundred of these conversations that I have had with Mahfouz since the end of 1994, as a tribute to the man on his ninetieth birthday. Their subjects are as diverse as the topics of the day over the years. But like his recent short stories, they carry the wisdom of the great man at this time of his life.

Mohamed Salmawy

Life Now

Sidi Gaber

I usually fall asleep only with the aid of sleeping pills, but this year on my birthday it was as if my body was celebrating the beginning of its ninetieth year in this world. After waking up in the morning, I nodded off again and slept peacefully all day, without the aid of sleeping pills. On normal days, this is so unheard of that it really did feel like a celebration.

The journey of life—well, with the approach of my ninetieth year I feel I am passing the penultimate station, Sidi Gaber station, as it were. When I went to Alexandria by train, I would always get off at Mahattat Masr, the last station on the line. So when I passed Sidi Gaber station I could afford the comfort of knowing that I wasn't getting off quite yet. But I also knew that I was edging closer and closer to Mahattat Masr, that it wouldn't be long before I had to pack my luggage and get ready to exit the train. This is what my birthday feels like this year: it is like passing Sidi Gaber station on the train.

14 December 2000

Taking Stock

I am still unable to talk about the emotional impact of the attempt on my life. Of course, man is the product of the experiences through which he passes, though the impact of those experiences takes some time to surface.

After the incident, five months ago, I was confined in hospital. Now I am confined to my home, where I am still having physiotherapy on my right arm. But I think I will never come to grasp the true impact of the attack.

Perhaps one reason for this is that I feel it happened to somebody else. I did not see the act happening. Had I seen the man who attacked me, were I able to remember the act of extending my hand to shake his (as I was told I did), the incident would have left a deeper impression. But all I can remember is sitting in the car, then turning to speak to my friend. And it is a blessing from God that we should develop such selective amnesia, since the details of such frightful situations would make life unbearable were they to remain vivid in the memory.

Of course I am aware of the material effects of this incident on my life. In the hospital I met with a great deal of love and care, showered on me by a great number of people. To these people I owe an immense debt of gratitude. I had not realized just how many people cared for me. But other than this, no, I cannot assess the impact of that event.

15 March 1995

Pen Friends

For the past three years—ever since I was attacked, on 14 November 1994—I have been under constant medical treatment. The past three years have been years of suffering. I have been unable to watch television or read, and I can no longer write with my right hand.

In these three years, I have had a new and significant experience, one which has brightened my days. I have discovered the real meaning of friendship. All my life, I have been surrounded by friends, but I only discovered what good friends they were after my accident. It is thanks to my friends that I have survived these years. Their love and care have sustained me day after day.

It may be a bit late for New Year's resolutions, but I do have one wish. I hope that my hand heals completely, and that I will be able to go back to writing, even small texts. I crave the feel of the pen between my fingers, if only to jot down a few words. I know that I cannot produce a literary work if I do not have the pen in my hand; I cannot dictate a novel. The meaning and significance of the words is, for me, inextricably linked with the movement of the pen on paper. As the ink flows, my ideas come, one after the other. Verbal expression, on the other hand, is difficult, perhaps because I am unaccustomed to saying words I can easily write.

I have indeed started writing, but I am only able to note a few words, more to exercise my hand than to express myself. I hope that in the coming year I will be able to write once more.

8 January 1998

Writing Now

I am undergoing physiotherapy, but my hand simply does not work as well as it used to. This has made writing an especially difficult and laborious process, which requires a real physical effort. In the past, it was as natural as walking: I did not think consciously about wrapping my fingers around the pen, taking it up, and guiding it along the page. People do not think consciously about putting one foot in front of the other; it is a spontaneous movement. The nerve centers send signals to the muscles, and the feet carry the body forward in a smooth, carefree manner.

The act of writing used to be the same for me. I would think about words or concepts or ideas, not about pushing my pen along a sheet of paper. Now, however, writing itself requires a good deal of concentration, if I am to form legible words running in more or less straight lines. The effort I make to form the letters reminds me of learning to write all over again.

This, of course, means that I am completely unable to work for hours at a stretch, as I used to do every day. I have the energy to write a few paragraphs, so the topics I choose to write about have to be compatible with such brevity: Mainly, I now write very short and concentrated stories. I have been writing such short stories for a long time, but they were once the fruit only of artistic necessity. This is not the case today.

23 September 1999

A Decade On

During the year that followed my winning the Nobel prize in 1988, I basked in happiness, but the decade since then has been a time for paying back this debt. The Nobel gave great impetus to my work, and to Arabic literature in particular; in material terms, it put my anxieties about my small family's future to rest. Because I was already well on in years when I received it, however, I have suffered several illnesses since, and have felt weak in general. I had to undergo heart surgery in London in 1990—a very difficult experience. Then I had another operation a few years later, which was equally tiresome. My sight and hearing have both declined quite drastically: I can no longer see more than a few centimeters' distance, and I hear very little: those who speak to me know what great efforts they must exert if they are to make themselves heard!

I never thought I would be able to live without the things I have enjoyed all my life: reading, for instance, watching the news on television and perusing the newspapers, or listening to music. These were my life's greatest pleasures. Now, I can no longer savor my favorite works, discover what is being written today by the new generation of writers, or listen to the music I love so much. Nor can I claim to have entered the modern world, since I cannot use a computer.

Yet ultimately, I thank God for everything: the long years I have lived have been good, even if, at this point, I have had to pay the price for my age.

15 October 1998

First-Hand Experience

I have read voraciously throughout my life. Every time I was interested in a subject—and my interests were always diverse—I would read everything I could lay my hands on, however remotely related. I would go to the National Library to read the classics, and regularly frequented the bookstores that sold works in modern literature. I read novels, of course, but also history, philosophy, politics, science .... Human curiosity is limitless, but one life is nowhere near enough to satisfy it.

Today, my age does not allow me to read as I used to. My health is not good enough for me to investigate the different topics that interest me. I neither see nor hear as well as I used to, and therefore I cannot follow up on current events or developments in world art and literature.

Friends read the newspapers to me every day, and on Fridays or holidays one of my daughters takes over this task. Apart from this, I am completely isolated from life, although I do ask my friends about what is going on in the world when they come to visit me. Books, music, and art continue to fascinate me, and the sense of knowing a little about new trends is very important to my well-being, both physical and mental. So I always ask, if only to feel that I am part of things. Still, I do not always receive a satisfactory response: to experience things at a remove, as it were, through someone else's eyes and ears, is not at all the same as feeling, hearing, and seeing them for oneself.

23 March 2000

Smoking

In this age of health-conscious living, even mentioning cigarettes is taboo. I only smoke three cigarettes a day, but my history as a smoker is a long one. I started smoking in my first year of secondary school; I remember I would hide my cigarettes and go to an empty lot where we played football. There I would sit for a while and have a smoke. It makes me laugh to think how long ago that was: imagine, I have been smoking for more than seventy years!

I am a moderate smoker, though, as I said: I am always amazed at people who smoke two or three packs a day. Smoking, for me, is a pleasure. I have never chain-smoked, that's for sure. I wait until I really long for a cigarette, and then I really enjoy it, unlike people who smoke as if they were eating the cigarette, or those who smoke non-stop because they are nervous. Smoking, for them, cannot be an enjoyable experience: it is a compulsion, or a bad habit, like biting your nails. I don't have the urge to light one cigarette after another. Some of my friends have said I actually check my watch before lighting a cigarette, to make sure it's time for another one.

There was only one period of my life during which I smoked a pack a day, but that was an exceptional time.

As for the *shisha*, that I learned to smoke at al-Fishawi, the coffeeshop in al-Husayn. Sometimes, I used to go to the Azbakiya Gardens and buy a ticket; with that, plus one piaster, I would have one of the excellent *shisha*s they prepared.

6 May 1999

Weighing the Past

When people inquire how I celebrate my birthday, I say that as a child, growing up in al-Husayn, birthdays were never celebrated. Only in later life did I come to realize that they could be a cause for celebration.

I cannot remember a single birthday celebration as I was growing up, and did not even know the birth dates of either of my parents or of my brothers or sisters. Only religious celebrations, such as Mulid al-Nabi and Ashura, were marked in our household.

Later, among the regulars at the Harafish meetings, we decided that whenever a birthday coincided with the weekly get-together, then that get-together should be sort of a celebration. This was the idea of the satirist Muhammad Afifi. We celebrated, among others, the birthdays of Ahmad Baha al-Din and Salah Jahin. And well after I had passed my half century, we celebrated my birthday for the first time.

Today, on the occasion of my birthday, I look back over the years that have passed and cannot help but feel that they stretch perhaps a little too far. But when I examine the past I am happy to report that hard work and perseverance have indeed furnished results. My labors have brought fruits alongside catastrophes that stem from the same efforts. Yet I remain content in the knowledge that the past has been fated, and if I were to compile a balance sheet I feel, in all honesty, that the gains would outweigh the losses.

5 December 1996

Suits You, Sir

At most, there are nine or ten winter suits hanging in my wardrobe. This is a large number, I hasten to add; many winters have gone by when I have not worn any of them more than once, and I am not the kind of person who gets excited about a new suit.

My tailor was a man I had heard of from my friend, the writer Tharwat Abaza, who came to me in a huff one day and pronounced these enigmatic words: "Only ten pounds stand between you and Délia." I replied, somewhat perplexed: "And who or what would Délia happen to be?"

Tharwat Abaza smiled. "Only the best tailor in Egypt," he informed me. "And he charges a mere ten pounds more than you are currently paying your tailor to make the finest suit you will ever have worn. Why not get him to make you a decent suit? Make no mistake, though: he is a very important man, and will not make a suit for just anyone, but you don't need to worry, because I'll put in a good word for you."

After that, Délia became a dear friend. A few years ago, he had to undergo surgery. I went to visit him in hospital. As I was wishing him a speedy recovery, he put his head on my shoulder and began to weep. That was the last time I saw him; he died soon afterward, and I stopped having suits made.

As for ties, I stopped wearing those a long time ago. At first, I made no special effort to avoid wearing a tie, and simply wore a roll-neck pullover. But even when I wasn't wearing garments that hid the neck area, I soon found I could not go back to wearing a tie. It was too constricting—I just couldn't bear it, nor could I see the reason why it was important. Besides, I could never get the hang of tying that particular noose.

Some of my friends, especially Yusuf al-Siba'i (may he rest in peace), would come to visit me and bring me ties when they returned from a trip abroad. But after a few such attempts, I asked them to forgive me for not wearing their gifts, and they soon gave up.

3 January 2000

Time the Reaper

I have been plunged into grief recently, due to the death of my older brother's son. He was a retired major-general, over seventy, but I still remember how I used to carry him on my shoulder when he was a small child.

What increases my pain is the fact that I find myself unable to attend the funeral or even pay my respects to his family in person. My health does not allow me to go out as much as I would have liked to, and there are also security considerations. Nor can I take part in any public gatherings.

I have had to apologize more times than I care to remember because I could not attend an event organized in my honor or other occasions, whether joyous or sad, involving people who are close to me.

The strange thing is that the deceased's father and mother, as well as his grandparents on both sides, enjoyed very long lives—some of them lived to see their hundredth birthday. Two of his brothers died before him, however, and they had not yet reached retirement age.

At any rate, such is God's will. Death comes when it comes. All we can do is think of this world, and of humanity, which lives and dies in the space of a breath. I sit here, pondering these matters, and my sadness seems about to overwhelm me at times.

My older brother's sons were very close to me. I played with them when they were children. The last time I saw the one who died recently was when he came to visit me in the hospital, at the time of that unfortunate incident.

11 May 2000

Another Birthday

At this stage of my life, I really feel it is a little silly to plan for the future. Looking back on my life I admit to feeling a degree of satisfaction. In all honesty, I feel that I accomplished what I could, and in the right way. But the truth of the matter is that I am ready to give up the ghost! I feel satiated with life and the only thing that relieves the oppression of the days is the knowledge that they pass.

The most important thing in my life now is friendship. Without my friends the last few years would have been the most miserable of my life. As for my readers, of whom I am so proud, all I wrote was for them, and will remain for them, whether I am alive or not. But my years have been a journey rich in good and bad.

People cannot resist asking what I have had from life. Well, like everyone else, I have had pain and pleasure. So in a sense I can say that I have had everything out of life it is possible to get. What I am most happy with is what I received from my fellow countrymen. The sincere appreciation I receive is, in my eyes, the greatest honor the world could heap on me. Their joy in my success was an unadulterated pleasure.

14 December 1995

My Friends

Friendship is not based on self-interest or on other selfish motives. Friends simply enjoy each other's company. Anything can be imposed on people, including marriage, the one exception to this rule being friendship. For friendship can only develop when there is a sense of spiritual closeness. Such closeness is the solid base upon which friendship is built; its existence guarantees that no obstacle will prove insuperable. Friendships develop between men and women. They develop across generations, between people of different cultures and traditions.

Take the circle of the Harafish as an example. We all differed in our views and outlooks on life but we were all united by a love of art. That was our common ground, which replaced the shared interest in politics that had originally tied the group together.

Recently an old friend who had lived in the United States for many years attended one of our meetings. He said that while he was away the thing that he had missed the most was the company of close friends, and their pleasant evening conversation. He regretted that abroad there is no time for friendship. When you call people they ask you immediately what you want. People are suspicious, it seems, of contact for the sake of contact.

Friendship is one of the great pleasures of life. And as you age it becomes, if anything, even more important.

7 March 1996

Writing Again

I have a special wish for the new year. I hope that my right arm heals completely, so that I may go back to real writing—sitting at my desk and writing for hours on end. My desire to write has not abated at all during the past few years. My mind is crowded with ideas, but my right hand still refuses to hold the pen. As for dictation, I use it for letters or newspaper articles, but in literary work, the impulses go straight from the heart to the hand, and I know of no other way to express my ideas.

Some writers were able to express themselves without putting pen to paper. Taha Husayn is an example; but he had dictated all his life, and did not have to start learning to use a new technique when he was eighty-five. I also know of writers who have learned to work on a computer instead of with a piece of paper and a pencil, but the time to learn new skills is long past for me. For more than half a century, I have been used to writing by hand, and in writing I have poured my very heart out. 'Writing'—expressing my ideas and thoughts—is, for me, the moment when the ink begins to flow through the pen and onto the paper. I know of no other way.

2 January 1997

Days Gone By

Moveable Feasts

I remember the first time my father gave me money—a gold pound—for the feast. Although the glittering coin was worth only 97.5 piasters, while the paper pound was a real pound, worth 100 piasters, I was overjoyed. I've heard, but find it hard to believe, that the gold pound is worth LE300 today. Things have changed so much! My father's gift was certainly not the only one I received on a feast day. Uncles and relatives also gave me gold pounds.

Had I known that the value of the gold pound would rise so, I would never have let go of my gifts. But normally, by the end of the feast, nothing remained in my pocket. During our outings to al-Husayn on feast days, we pampered ourselves, eating all the goodies that caught our fancy: Turkish delight stuffed with cream, *couscous*, candied apples. The clothes with which we refused to part the night before the feast had the smell of new fabric. I recall an outfit I received when I was ten or twelve. I loved it, and always associated it with happy times. I kept it until it disintegrated.

On ordinary days, I usually went with my childhood friends to the cinema by tram. But one feast day, we decided to treat ourselves to a film at the Cinema Cosmograph (the present Cosmo). It was frequented by foreigners at the time. We even took a horse-drawn carriage. But the carriage hit a child, and we spent the rest of the day at the police station.

29 January 1998

Happy Eid

Nobody feels the joy of the Eid as much as children, and when we were children, we could hardly contain our excitement while waiting for it: pocket money, new outfits, new shoes. We would put on these valuable garments and go out to show them off to the other children of the neighborhood.

We would also show off our mothers' *kahk* (the Eid confection par excellence), all the different varieties, so that instead of having one helping, each of us would get five or six. The last time I ate *kahk* was a long time ago. When I became diabetic I stopped eating sweets, though I had a liking for them

That is the way of life. You give up your pleasures one by one until there is nothing left, then you know it is time to go.

28 December 2000

My Friend the Sheep

This [Mahfouz points to a spot on the edge of his forehead] is my oldest memory of the Eid. I was five years old, maybe six. It was my family's habit to buy a sheep some weeks before the Eid and look after it until it was slaughtered. In the interim, a relationship would develop between myself and the sheep: I would feed it and play with it and, one day, having decided I was a musketeer, the sheep my valiant steed, determined that I would ride it. Now was my chance to make real some of the scenes I had watched endlessly at the cinema. I straddled the sheep and held onto its horns with both hands. And the poor creature, naturally, tossed its head back. I was thrown onto the floor. It was a big wound, and I never forgot the bleeding.

And yet the incident had no effect on my friendship with the sheep. I decided to let it go, assuming that it was the sheep equivalent of joking that had gone too far, as it often does among childhood friends. When the sheep was slaughtered, that was the saddest moment for me, not least because it was a moment of irrevocable separation after weeks of growing familiarity and attachment. That grief became a yearly predicament, but then when the family assembled at the dining table—I sometimes refused to join them at first—the smell of grilled lamb took my mind off it.

8 March 2001

Games of Yesterday

Between the ages of seven and ten I remember taking great care to meet daily with my friends in al-Husayn. So much so that it seems to me now that I have lost touch with them all. Indeed, though I remember family names, there is only one of my early playmates whose first name I remember.

He was the son of a police commissioner in al-Gamaliya. His name was Hammam. Though we subsequently lost touch some relatives have told me that he is now a judge. I remember visiting his family with my mother in their house near the police station. Hammam and I used to play in the square next to his house, which at that time was perfectly safe since there were no motor vehicles.

The square was like a playground. I remember how we used to wait for the cart that twice daily would cross the square, pulled by two mules. With the other children, I would run happily after it.

When I was ten we moved to Abbasiya and my circle of friends expanded. At the same time I began to show an interest in sports, particularly football. I remained in touch with members of the team, some of whom I still meet, though sadly most of them have now passed away.

8 February 1996

Once, in the Desert

Critics over the years have often produced innovative interpretations of my works, finding entirely new themes. One critic, for example, has interpreted the Nile in my books as representing the worldly and the sensuous, and the desert as purity and spirituality.

During my childhood days in Abbasiya, I recall the large expanse of desert known as Ard al-Uyun. For us, as children, it was the Mulid al-Nabi Desert, since we knew it as the venue for the *mulid* festivities every year. On other days of the year, the land was just an arid expanse of desert. I often spent time there to meditate or read poetry. I enjoyed the dry desert climate, and the sea of sand stretched endlessly before my eyes. But once the sun set, I hurriedly set off home, afraid of what desert creatures might make their appearance after sunset.

In this area was a plot of land that we used as a football pitch. We split ourselves into two teams. When we competed in tense and exciting games, the residents of Abbasiya would come to cheer for one team or the other. The desert of my childhood was located between the eastern part of Abbasiya and an area where tombs were being built at the time. This area is today the Madafin al-Ghafir ('Watchman's Tombs'). The desert of my childhood has disappeared. It has become a busy area of Abbasiya, covered with buildings and bustling with life.

1 April 1999

Childish Histrionics

I was happy to learn that, in the past year alone, fifty new film theaters have been built in Egypt. I was reminded of the cinema I used to go to as a child at the beginning of the last century, the Cinema Bayt al-Qadi, which was located close to our house in Khan Gaafar. That was probably the oldest movie theater in the country. Even when we moved to Abbasiya, I would take my friends and show them where I had gone as a boy. Sometimes the cinema would be shut, its owner would be lounging about in the adjoining café, and we would pay him the price of a ticket and ask him to open his cinema and play something for us, usually a Charlie Chaplin film. I saw the same repertoire of two or three silent movies over and over and over, but I never got bored.

By the time we moved to Abbasiya, other, more modern theaters had opened up elsewhere and I started going to them, but I never forgot Bayt al-Qadi.

I loved the cinema as a child, so much that often they had to get me out of the theater by force because I would have been perfectly willing to live there. In order to go to the cinema, I would have to be chaperoned by an old retainer. When we took our seats in the auditorium she would fall asleep almost instantly, while I perked up for the magic unfolding before me on the screen.

12 April 2001

Childhood Cinemas

Following my stint at Cinema Bayt al-Qadi, I relocated to more modern venues, showing newer, better films, like Cinema Olympia and Cinema Ideal. This was a major step forward for me.

I loved cinema so much I actually bought a little cinema comprising a candle-operated projector: rapt, my friends and I would switch off the lights and watch the images flickering on one wall. The films were bought outside Cinema Olympia, I remember. When I started going there, it was my first experience of being part of a culturally oriented group, which opened my eyes to various disciplines besides cinema, including literature and art. I recall clearly that little film shop, its owner sitting quietly inside it, just like somebody who sells books.

None of this survives now. When I compare those films with the videos and CD-ROMs of today, I reflect how simple and basic my own equipment was. Yet it excited me, I suspect, more than its counterparts excite the young men and women of the present day. And there is so much I remember. One popular French comedy—the cult classic of my generation—is so vivid in my mind I could actually have watched it yesterday, believe it or not.

19 April 2001

Show Me a Child

When I was a child there really was an absence of children's books. It was not then an established genre, and so children in my day, if they read, were forced to read books for adults. Initially I read crime novels—cops and robbers, that kind of thing—though later I turned to romantic novels, which proved as worthless as police stories.

All the books I read were translated into Arabic. For a while I was under the impression that this was because, somehow, they were important literary texts. Later I discovered just how erroneous was this belief.

One character in a series of crime novels, I remember, was called Son of Johnson. A strange name, I thought, even at the time. It was only later that I discovered that this character was in fact invented by the translator Hafez Naguib, who had earlier had a great success with a translation of a series of novels about a thief called Johnson. In order to capitalize on this earlier success, Hafez Naguib had created the character's son.

Such was the popularity of translated novels that the translator's invention was by no means unique. The covers of books often bore misleading information: novels written in Egypt, in Arabic, would often have "Translated from the French" emblazoned across their dust-jackets.

Actual translations were often just as misleading, and I well remember being amazed at the familiar manner in which Guy de Maupassant would introduce the Prophet's *hadith* in his novels.

17 August 1995

...ords

...studied during the holy ... this was the month ... at any other time. My ... do with my studies, ... month, greater than at ... I could give free rein ... school literature.

... that I never wrote ... during the summer ... thus gained one ... to one month less when ...

On ... read the whole of the Ho... very special reading, very different from re... er year I read the *Life of t...* ... remember reading *Selected ...* ..., Sheikh al-Sakandari, and Ali ... contained selections of Arabic poetry and prose from the pre-Islamic era to modern times. I also read al-Zayyat's *History of Arabic Literature*, as well as a book I greatly treasured containing brief outlines on the histories of Sufi sheikhs and selections of their writings. I remember that during my first years at university I read plays by Bernard Shaw, the poems of T.S. Eliot, and any new publications by al-Aqqad and al-Mazni. I read the *Islamiyat* of al-Aqqad and Taha Husayn's autobiography.

1 February 1997

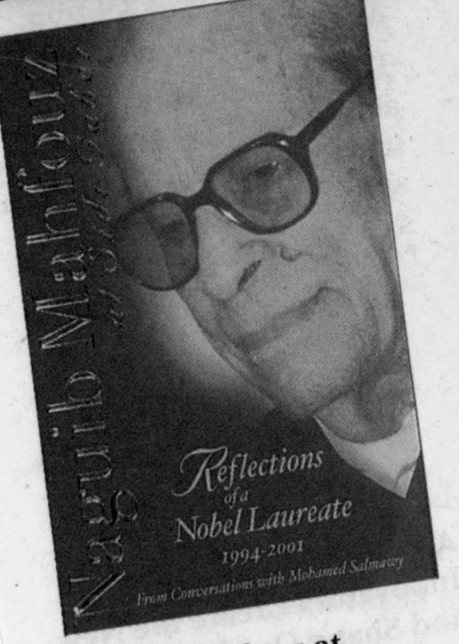

Naguib Mahfouz at Sidi Gaber: Reflections of a Nobel Laureate, 1994–2001.
Naguib Mahfouz from conversations with Mohamed Salmawy.
Published in the aftermath of the 1994 stabbing incident that almost cost him his life, the Nobel Prize–winning author offers a collection of views and observations of his native Egypt and the world at large. Pub. 4/02. 5 1/8x8 in. 156 pp.

Fifteen Days

Fresh from university, I was employed in the Ministry of Religious Endowments when Abd al-Salam al-Shazli was minister. A martinet for discipline, he decided to reform the ministry. He issued an order to close the gate at eight sharp every morning. Anyone absent by eight o'clock had a day cut from his annual holidays. Should he be late a second time, then fifteen days' pay would be deducted from his salary.

Members of the public were forbidden to enter the ministry and would be interviewed by the head of the Investigation Department at the gate. The inspector would then contact the civil servant responsible for the matter. A date would be fixed for the petitioner's return and should the civil servant not have completed any business related to the case by this date, a full fifteen days' pay would be deducted.

No food was allowed into the ministry, and the reading of newspapers was banned. Anyone found eating or reading had . . . yes, fifteen days' pay deducted.

I was parliamentary secretary to Shazli Pasha, and on one occasion had prepared a written reply for the minister to deliver to the assembly. I handed him the envelope and then sat outside the office to reread a short story of mine that I had just completed. To my horror, I found that I had the text of the reply in my hands. The story was in the envelope. I rushed into Shazli Pasha's office before he entered the chamber and exchanged the two envelopes when the minister seemed distracted.

Hooliganism Today

When we were children, we would often see pitched battles between two groups of thugs. But as soon as a policeman arrived on the scene, the fight would come to an abrupt halt. You would see a scrawny little policeman, fresh off the train from the countryside, ordering gigantic men about, as if herding a flock of sheep.

I witnessed the end of the era of hooliganism, and I saw the thugs, who were a terrifying sight to contemplate when they had worked up a rage during their fights. A policeman would always intervene, however, shouting, "Quick march to the Wayli police station!" The policemen carried no weapons, but commanded respect to a degree you cannot imagine. This made it possible for us to stroll fearlessly, late at night, in the empty streets of Abbasiya.

The situation is obviously very different today. The strong men of the past would never have thought of attacking the forces of law and order, but now I hear that security forces are being attacked. This is entirely unacceptable.

I condemn organized violence, whether it takes the form of terrorism or of hooliganism. But the confrontation in which we must engage must include the development and improvement of the judicial system. Lengthy litigation processes lead many people to despair of ever seeing justice done, and therefore some resort to extrajudicial means in order to obtain what they believe is their right.

21 August 1997

Vicious Circle

That group of friends of mine, the Harafish (after which my novel about the marginalized underclass, the 'riffraff,' was named), used to meet, first, in a café overlooking the Nile, opposite what was to become President Sadat's residence. At that time, this area was almost entirely abandoned, and we would sit in a circle on the grass with the Nile directly before us, talking for hours, discussing our troubles to the end.

This is how we eventually came to refer to that place as the Vicious Circle, because of the circle in which we usually sat, but more importantly because we spoke of nothing but our frustration at that time. Political conditions were very painful prior to the Revolution, beset by corruption, bribery, and political fumbling against the backdrop of the British occupation. It all weighed heavily on us; moreover, nobody had any genuine sympathy for us or understood our situation, which carried the collective frustration into our personal lives.

Of the Harafish, many subsequently stopped writing or emigrated. The reason I stayed is that I liked writing more than I liked what it seemed apt to give rise to: money and fame. If these things came along, it would be wonderful. But I functioned mostly as if they had already come, because my true happiness and joy were in the writing itself.

1 February 2001

Change of Seasons

I am at my most productive in the autumn and winter. Unlike many species that hibernate during winter, my spirit opens up. But when spring comes along I begin what I call my summer hibernation.

In the spring of 1934, the year I graduated from university, I suffered from various allergies that effected my eyes and skin. Every spring the allergies would reappear and I was virtually incapacitated and unable to work. Hence, autumn became my season of recuperation, a season that continued to the end of winter.

I never associated winter with illness, whether influenza or any other malady. This is the reason for my love of autumn and winter. Even now I find summer a trial. I usually go through the summer months fighting depression, anxiously awaiting winter.

When I was younger I used to consider summer a total waste of time since I could write barely a word. Now I look back with some gratitude to summer as a season of forced rest. Without that rest I would have gone on writing endlessly, and that would probably have made me tire of my work, eventually leading me to give it up. It was my enforced halt over the summer that always made me return to work with greater anticipation and excitement.

9 November 1995

A Mother's Love

I was lucky enough to get my fill of my mother's affection and tenderness, for God allowed her to live until I was in my fifties. During all the times when one really needs a mother and the special quality of the love only she can give, my mother was there for me. I can't imagine what it must be like to grow up without that kind of tenderness—one must feel an aching void all one's life. Don't believe it if someone says, "Oh, So-and-so was just like a mother to me." This is merely a metaphor. No one can really take a mother's place.

Before my mother's death, I had already experienced the loss of someone dear: my father, who passed away when I was twenty-five. Although I was closer to my mother than to him, his death came as an immense shock: this was the first time death had snatched someone from my family. This experience marked me deeply, coming as it did during my formative years.

It is true, as people say, that one only attains maturity with the death of one's mother. As long as she was alive, I depended on my mother for many things—not for material things, but for emotional support. With her gone, I came to feel that I was truly alone in the world. I had friends, to be sure, and my own family: but the place my mother had occupied was empty forever. Many young people today leave their families as soon as they have finished school, and assume full responsibility for their own welfare. In these cases, the loss of a parent is not such a crushing blow. The world has changed so much.

27 May 1999

Inspired from Afar

I was very pleased to hear of the museum in Alexandria devoted to the works of the great painter Mahmud Said. I had a wonderful relationship with him, although we never knew each other.

In the late 1920s, I was in my last years of school. I read an article by al-Aqqad about a painter called Mahmud Said, and was amazed. Art, at the time, did not play a very important role in society, so it was surprising that the great al-Aqqad himself should devote an entire article to an artist.

I asked several people about this, and was told that men of literature are not concerned with *belles lettres* alone, but must study all the arts: painting, sculpture, music . . . . From them, he may draw inspiration.

Mahmud Said was the person who introduced me to the world of the plastic arts, the world of canvas and charcoal and paint. I later learned that one collective exhibition a year was held on Ibrahim Pasha Street in Cairo, but there were individual exhibitions as well that one could attend. At the collective exhibitions, which I began to frequent every year, I saw Mahmud Said's work for the first time. That first vision is still imprinted on my mind, the colors as bright as they were when I first beheld them. Part of his genius lay in the fact that he found and uncovered beauty where no one else had seen it: in the splendid, statuesque working-class women whose portraits made him famous, for instance. No one had done that before him.

Mahmud Said was truly a great man, I realized this when I saw his work, but also when I found out he had been a magistrate, but had left the law and devoted all his time to art. So in other words, he had left one of the most respected positions in the society of the day to become an artist. That fact played a great part in my decision, many years later, to abandon philosophy, which I had studied at university, and make literature my main muse.

2 April 2000

Worlds of Art

After my exhilarating first encounter with the works of Mahmud Said, I became interested in art, passionately so. I bought a book—which I still have—titled *Outline of Art*. It is a basic sort of book, which traces the history of world art in a very enjoyable way for the novice, and covers just about everything from the pharaohs to Picasso.

I remember that every morning, I would enjoy one picture, as if it were the day's first cup of coffee. Starting the day that way was wonderful. After I had dressed, and before going to work, I would turn over a new page and contemplate a new painting, which would stay with me all day long. It could be Toulouse Lautrec's *Le Moulin Rouge*, or a bas-relief from a pharaonic temple, or Van Gogh's *Sunflowers*.

This is how I developed a very intense, very personal relationship with works that are clichés to most art aficionados. I felt they were mine alone; they set the rhythm of my day. I also felt strongly about al-Tilmisani's collection—he was a good friend of mine, and I followed his surrealist work, as well as that of Ramses Yunan and Fuad Kamel. They put out a very enjoyable magazine in which I published a few things. Al-Tilmisani had a wide-ranging knowledge of cultural matters and the library of a man of letters.

I was also interested in music, and did my best to acquaint myself with it. Again, I had a favorite book—which I perused endlessly. I would read about the great classic pieces, then listen to them, entranced.

27 January 2000

Saturn Rising

The year 1943 marked the beginning of my lifelong association with publishing. Together with my friends, I was keen to find a publisher for some short stories we had written. Later, this circle of friends came to be called the Harafish. Ahmad Mazhar, Thabet Amin, Amin al-Dahabi, and Mahmud Shabana joined the group, which used to meet regularly in our favorite place, Casino Opera.

Various artists were drawn to the group. Eventually we ended up spending many pleasant evenings in Muhammad Afifi's home. At that point the group was more than twenty strong and included Salah Jahin, Mustafa Mahmud, Ahmad Baha al-Din, and Louis Awad.

The events of one particular Thursday evening remain fresh in my mind. On that day Salah Jahin informed us that he was getting married the following Thursday. Mustafa Mahmud turned his eyes skyward, and claimed he could see Saturn rising, which he interpreted as an inauspicious sign. We simply laughed the matter off.

Three days before Jahin's proposed wedding a far greater event occurred, the ramifications of which were to overshadow our Thursday meetings for years to come. That day was Monday, 5 June 1967. When, later, we met with Jahin, he made no more mention of his marriage.

22 February 1996

The Nobel and Other Awards

Nobel Intentions

The Nobel prize made no difference to who I am as a person. There was, of course, the pride in being so honored, but a laureate remains a writer first and foremost. A Nobel never created a writer out of a void. All one has to fall back on is one's own capacities and talents, whatever these may be. The prize simply constitutes recognition of one's work and its value. Sometimes great writers are not recognized in this way. When I met the great American playwright Arthur Miller, he described the Nobel as an accident that could happen to a writer.

Of course, sometimes recipients are not exceptional. They shine for a moment, then sink back into the relative anonymity in which they had lived. Perhaps this is due in part to changes in literary taste, not to the writer's lack of talent. Fads change quickly and what was popular yesterday is often denigrated today. Many great writers are not read in their lifetime, simply because another genre was popular during that particular period. When tastes change again, such writers may be rediscovered and read with amazement at their literary prowess. Such a 'discovery,' however, may come too late for the writer to enjoy.

In this perspective, literary prizes can come to pluck little-known writers from obscurity, and allow them to bask in the glow of recognition.

24 November 2000

From Afar

Although I never knew him personally, Abbas al-Aqqad had a profound impact on my life. A competition for story-writing was held once, and most of the jury was quite traditional. None of the members thought much of new literary trends—except for Abd al-Qader al-Mazni. The jury awarded the prize that year to Muhammad Said al-Erian, for his novel *Bab Zuwayla*. But al-Mazni disagreed, and said that the jury could not disregard the novel I had entered in the competition. They refused to award the prize to my novel *New Cairo*, saying that it was too bold: for one thing, its hero was a pimp. The jury also found *Midaq Alley* beyond the pale. So al-Mazni asked them, "Well, what about *Khan al-Khalili*?"

While they were discussing this, they began to raise their voices. At this moment, al-Aqqad was passing. He asked them why they were fighting and they told him: "We can't come to an agreement, so you decide. We want to give the prize to *Bab Zuwayla*, and al-Mazni wants to divide it between that and *Khan al-Khalili*." I was told that al-Aqqad, after having read both novels, sent to the jury to say that he disagreed with both opinions: he thought the author of *Khan al-Khalili* alone should be awarded the prize. So the jury agreed to divide it.

A few years before his death, in an interview on television, he also said I deserved the Nobel. He was the first to predict I would receive it.

22 July 1999

My First Prize

I will always remember the first award I received: the Qut al-Qulub al-Dimardashiya Prize. It came at the beginning of my literary career and you cannot imagine how this prize encouraged me to follow the path I had chosen. It was the first sign of recognition by the critics of the time that I was on the right path.

The prize was LE40, to be shared between myself and Ali Ahmad Bakathir—I for my novel *Rhadopis*, he for his novel *Peasant Woman*, which was later made into a film starring Umm Kulthum. All Abbasiya enjoyed my LE20, which I spent on the young people in the area. Those twenty pounds were limitless. Whenever friends noticed me wearing a new pair of shoes, they would say, "*Rhadopis*," and if I bought a cheese sandwich, they would also exclaim "*Rhadopis!*"

I never met the lady who offered the prize, as she left the choice to a committee including the most illustrious writers of the day, among them Dr. Taha Husayn and Ahmad Amin. I received my prize from them, although I did go to Qut al-Qulub's house to leave a word of thanks.

I was employed at the time by the Ministry of Religious Endowments, and was told that Ahmad Amin wanted to speak to me on the telephone. I answered quaking, but he was very affable and asked me whether, since I had written an historical novel, I had studied ancient Egyptian history, the subject of my novel. I replied that I had indeed studied Egyptian history very thoroughly. He then asked me why, in that case, I had written about pharaoh being driven in a cart pulled by horses? Did I not know that horses were only introduced into Egypt during the reign of the Hyksos several centuries later? I explained that I was aware of that fact, but in my novel I wanted to endow the pharaoh with the maximum of pomp and splendor. Ahmad Amin was able to explain this to the other members of the committee, who accepted that it was not a slip on my part but a modification, in the interest of the novel. So I won the prize.

23 October 1997

Youthful Prizes

Prizes have certainly had an impact on my career as a writer, particularly at the outset. When I began, it was extremely difficult to get a book published, so much so that whenever I finished a novel I would put the manuscript in some drawer, sometimes for years, before it found a publisher and the time came for it to see the light.

In fact, it was before any of my books were published that I received my first award, the Qut al-Qulub al-Dimardashiya prize. This was followed by prizes offered by the Arab Language Academy and the Ministry of Education. And I have no doubt that such awards paved the way toward the publication of my novels.

The Publication Committee for University Graduates, established by Abd al-Hamid Guda and Said al-Sahhar in 1943, was an important sponsor of new writers, and, emboldened by the prizes I had won, they proceeded to publish my writings.

It must be remembered that at the time winning a prize was an unquestionable recognition of the value of a work of fiction, and guaranteed, too, that it would find a ready readership among members of the public. Prizes then, were at that time an important aspect of the literary life of the nation.

2 September 1999

Other Awards

Every award I receive affects me as if it were the first. Each one gives a particular satisfaction, and leaves me feeling that I am appreciated, and so is my work. Unfortunately though, not every award of which I was the recipient has led to happier circumstances.

I well remember the first award I received after the July 1952 Revolution, the State Incentive Award, then worth LE1,000. I used the money as a down payment on a piece of land fronting the Nile, but unwittingly became entangled with a gang of crooks. I ended up without the money and without the land.

The State Merit Award I received after being proposed for seven consecutive years. I eventually received LE2,500, which I immediately paid in back taxes since the tax office had recently decided that the decree exempting artists from taxation did not cover the production of books.

The prize that gave me the greatest pleasure was the very first I received, which consisted of LE40 offered by Mme Qut al-Qulub al-Dimardashiya, and the reason for my pleasure was that I felt I had been finally accepted as a real writer.

The Nobel prize was unexpected. When my wife told me I had won, I thought she was joking until the doorbell rang and in walked a large foreigner. I asked him who he was, and he told me he was the Swedish Ambassador. It was then I realized that I had really won.

13 April 1995

My Cafés

Urabi's Café

While al-Fishawi, located in the heart of al-Husayn, has been the café most closely associated with my name, Qahwat Urabi, which once stood in Abbasiya was no less dear to me.

The café was owned by Ma'allim Urabi, once one of the strong men *(futuwwa)* of al-Husayniya. He opened the café after serving a sentence in prison. The café was frequented by an illustrious clientele. In his heyday, when he was in control, Urabi, like all the *futuwwat* of his time, must have rendered services to prominent figures, probably during election campaigns.

The café was well managed and impeccably clean. There were traditions and rituals to be observed: on entering, we had to go and greet Urabi. He would majestically rise to his feet, return our greeting, and invite us to enter the café. No one was allowed to sit down or order unless the ritual was fully performed. On feast days, the rich and famous could be seen placing gold pounds in the hands of the *ma'allim*'s children. The children were too young to spend the money, of course, and the gift was meant for the boss himself.

On feast days, when we performed the usual ritual, we would find Urabi sitting at his table, eating his feast day breakfast of broth and *fatta*. He would invariably invite us to share his meal, and we invariably thanked him and ordered our usual dish of *fuul* or smoked a *shisha*.

15 May 1997

Last Man Standing

Ma'allim Urabi, the owner of the coffeehouse I used to frequent, was jailed for a famous incident in Daher. On horseback, he led the *futuwwat* (strong men) of al-Husayniya in an assault on the Daher *futuwwat*, and closed down the whole quarter. It is said that Ma'allim Urabi personally gouged out the eyes of the leading *futuwwa* of Daher, and that the police had to intervene and seal off the area to terminate the battle. Ma'allim Urabi was given a twenty-year prison sentence. An end was put to the *futuwwat* protection system as a result of this incident: Ma'allim Urabi was the last of the *futuwwat*. He was eventually released on parole and became the owner of the coffeeshop I have mentioned.

All the *futuwwat* in my novels were based on different pictures of Ma'allim Urabi. I knew him only as a silent man, sitting quietly in his coffeeshop. I was always struck by the contrast between the tales I had heard about Ma'allim Urabi and the actual personality of the man after his release from prison. I frequented his coffeeshop until his death.

His children tried hard to run the coffeeshop in the same way as their father, but never succeeded. Before long they sold it off, and the place was turned into a furniture shop, thus bringing to an end a whole page of history.

22 May 1997

Coffee Club

For me, the café is the place where I used to meet my closest friends. Later, as a writer, the café became a place to meet other writers and intellectuals. But I also go to the café to be alone, to watch passersby and meditate. The café is where I smoke the *shisha*, an activity that would be unthinkable at home but that could take up the whole day at the café. At certain times, of course, all four of these elements were present at once.

I have been a regular at different cafés. As a young schoolboy, I would accompany my father to al-Club al-Masri. My father normally indulged in conversation with his friends, after ordering me a piece of Turkish delight or an ice cream.

When in secondary school, I started frequenting cafés with my friends. We would have a hard time deciding between Qushtumur and the café just opposite it, Isis, of which no trace remains today. We even dared to go to the Urabi café, known for its high-society clientele. But soon we moved to al-Husayn, to al-Fishawi. After that, we went to the café now named after me. It had been built on the site of a ruined monument. After my Nobel award, it was transformed by an architect and became the elegant place we know today.

11 December 1997

Coffee for Thought

The cafés I visited were for me as much cultural club as coffeeshop. In chronological order, the first of these cultural meeting places was Casino Opera, followed by Café Riche, Ali Baba Café, and Casino Qasr al-Nil. I was a regular client at the last one until my attack, after which I was advised not to sit at cafés.

There is a profound difference between cafés in the popular areas like al-Husayn and the elegant cafés of downtown Cairo. In the popular cafés, you do not need to have company beforehand, because as soon as you settle down into your chair, you can start making friends. In the elegant cafés, it is another matter. If you happen to be by yourself when you arrive, you will certainly also leave by yourself. For me and my friends, downtown cafés were only meeting places from which to move on, to the cinema or theater.

I have written a number of film scripts sitting at café tables. I wrote the script for a film directed by Salah Abu Seif as I sat in the Trianon in Alexandria, and the script for *Raya and Sakina* in a café in Glymenopoulos. But when it comes to literary writing, I can only go about the actual writing process if I am sitting at my desk. Ideas and characters, however, may very well have been developed from my experiences at the cafés that I hurriedly jotted down as soon as I got home. Al-Fishawi is certainly the café that inspired me the most.

18 December 19977

Alexandria Coffee

In Alexandria, in the summertime, I used to go to the café only to meet my friends. I often joined Tawfiq al-Hakim's group at Casino Petra. The Silsila district, I recall, was dotted with cafés. The Corniche cafés gave directly onto the sea, and each had its own special *shisha*. Smoking the *shisha* in Alexandria is especially enjoyable. The humid weather has the advantage of keeping the tobacco moist. In Cairo, the waiter must remove the pipe from time to time to wet the tobacco and bring it back so that it does not get too hot.

In Alexandria, I was also accustomed to sitting at Café Diana and the Louvre Café. The latter was bought by the late Abd al-Hamid al-Wakil after the 1952 Revolution. My visits there were driven by a nostalgia for the Wafd and the old party members who had all been Abd al-Hamid Bey's colleagues. The sight of them always filled me with an immense sense of serenity and tranquility. The Louvre's coffee was said to be the best in Alexandria. As for the food, it was cooked by Abd al-Hamid Bey's chef, who had been in his service in better days. The chef was entrusted with making the coffee and preparing the elaborate meals that otherwise graced only the dinner tables of the rich.

25 December 1997

Literature

The Idea

To me, a novel is a story through which characters are presented. Through the story and the characters, the outlines of a social, psychological, romantic, or political problem appear. There is always an idea behind a novel, at least behind the novel as I know it.

They say, however, that changes have come about: now, the important thing is the text in itself. How can this be? Unfortunately, I do not know, since I have been cut off from the pleasure of reading for a while now. So as far as I am concerned, a novel is still an idea, and a plot, and characters.

I can conceive, however, of a novel that does not tell a story, since several writers have dealt with a single situation, in which events do not follow a linear pattern of development. I can also imagine a novel without characters, peopled instead by names and meanings that have no psychological dimensions or specific personality traits. Yet I cannot even think of a novel not driven by an idea—unless we are talking about whodunits or mystery novels, where the plot is usually perfected to an extreme degree, and in which the characters are usually portrayed with incredible precision, but which do not go much further than that.

Literary works are quite different, and that is the difference between, say, *Crime and Punishment* and *Murder on the Orient Express*. That is why Agatha Christie's books must end with the arrest and the resolution of the mystery, while Dostoyevsky, in fact, could take that event as his starting point.

11 March 1999

Secret Reader

The ultimate goal of any writer is to satisfy both the elite and the average reader. Shakespeare's ideas may be profound, his characters of a complexity that must be studied, yet his plays are never wanting in humor and humanity. These traits make them accessible even to those who cannot understand the many references and allusions with which they are rife. Because of this uncanny ability to touch the cultured and the uneducated alike, Shakespeare's plays have universal appeal.

Other literary works are too difficult for average readers. The difficulty may be ascribed to the innovative approach of the writer. This approach may be worthy in itself, but the public is not familiar with it, and therefore fails to appreciate it. This does not imply that all works that become bestsellers are of uniformly high quality. One must not discount the mass appeal of the cheap thrill, which explains the wide audience catered to by writers of cloak-and-dagger mysteries, slasher horror stories, and pornography.

When I write, I simply feel that I am addressing myself. A writer must not feel that he is talking directly to the public—although, admittedly, the public is ever present in the back of his mind. If the readers are the writer's sole concern, he will sacrifice much and gain little. As he takes up his pen, a writer must think only of the work at hand, of himself, and possibly of another reader, identical to himself. Once that much is accomplished, he can only wait and hope for the best.

2 December 1999

Sufism and Poetry

Of course, aside from the realism with which Western criticism has concerned itself, if there is a spiritual dimension to writing—arising, as it would be, from the Sufi ether in which life in the East is constantly immersed—I am certainly aware of it, yes, but that does not mean that it is intentional or premeditated.

In fact, my aim has often been one of pure, unadulterated realism, but the inevitably poetic dramas of life in this part of the world, the poetry inherent to Arabic, and the poetry of the setting come through in spite of me.

Ultimately, of course, one's eyes never stray too far from the realist end in view, but while one is working toward that end, meandering down the path that will eventually conclude the story to be woven—in looking at Egypt's back streets and alleyways, the historic buildings, the architecture of time, and the transformations time has wrought on the architecture—one cannot help seeing the spirit that has always lived there, the soul that informs the body and endows it with meaning.

Perhaps this is a feature of all literature. Literature that does not rise to the level of poetry—whether it takes the form of verse or prose—bears no relation to literature at all.

18 January 2001

Forms of Ambiguity

Some people say that art and literature are becoming increasingly obscure and ambiguous. Many paintings, for instance, and many musical compositions, seem accessible only to the specialist.

This ambiguity may be due to many factors. One is the difficulty of the thought process itself, in cases where a writer seeks to convey a particularly complex idea to the reader. In these cases, the reader must make a special effort to understand the work, perhaps reading it more than once, or resorting to critical or analytical commentaries on the text. This is only natural for those who are not used to reading demanding literature.

The same can be said of music: if you are listening to Beethoven for the first time, you must read studies of his symphonies in order to absorb their many nuances. In other words, the impression of ambiguity or complexity here must be attributed to the audience itself, if it is unaccustomed to difficult art, which demands sustained concentration and a measure of background knowledge.

There are other cases, however, in which complexity is the fault of the writer, and not an inherent feature of the story or a deficiency in the reader. Here, the writer is incapable of conveying an idea with the necessary clarity. This is often a question of insufficient technique, which hinders fluency of expression.

Of course, there is the third factor, the worst of all, in which the writer intentionally envelopes his or her work in ambiguity, in the belief that readers will be impressed by anything incomprehensible.

25 November 1999

The Universal

There are no features that are the exclusive prerogative of good literature, beyond the comprehensiveness of the ideas in which it deals, and the depth and vision of the work.

Literary excellence is a standard that applies across national boundaries. The fact that a writer may not be known outside his home country does not affect the stature of that writer. Stature is, after all, determined by the work, not by the extent of its dissemination. Stature is not determined by the acquisition of awards.

The failure to win prizes cannot be held against any particular writer, nor can success be taken as a guarantee of quality. The picture is far more complex than this, and works of literature cannot be reduced to prize-giving citations.

As for localism, it is an inevitability, since the writer writes only of the reality he lives. Dostoyevsky, for instance, is a local writer. He takes the reader with him to the streets and quarters of old Moscow, with its characters and their problems. Yet no one can deny the universality of Dostoyevsky, a universality that is derived from the characteristics of the literature itself, not from the place where the events occur. Universality, then, has an aesthetic and not a topographical character.

28 December 1995

Unequal Distribution

Universality in literature implies two concepts, the first qualitative, the second quantitative. The latter implies a high level of acceptance among a diverse readership—something that might apply to, say, detective stories. Agatha Christie, we should remember, is translated into a vast number of languages and her books are available all over the world. She probably outsells all the literary genres put together.

The quantitative concept, then, implies a mass acceptance, the result of an equally massive distribution that has no bearing on literary worth or merit. Qualitative considerations, on the other hand, apply only to those works that afford some degree of intellectual satisfaction, regardless of questions related to their availability. Distribution, in terms of both quantity and geographical cover, is an inappropriate yardstick by which to measure quality.

A piece of literature can have a significance that is universal, even if it is restricted in the extent of its distribution. A print run of a few thousand copies may well contain something far more important—indeed is likely to contain something far more important—than whatever lies between the covers of a volume produced in units measured in multiples of a million or more. Agatha Christie, after all, has outsold Thomas Mann a hundredfold, yet the claims that we make for Mann are hardly applicable to the queen of crime. Quantity can never substitute for quality, nor should the two be confused.

21 December 1995

One-Shot Wonders

There are writers who publish one immensely successful novel, then sink once more into the oblivion from which they rose. If they do manage to produce another work, it is rarely anything like the first in terms of critical acclaim. This is usually due to the fact that the writer has been through a major experience or discovered something very new, so everyone wants to read all about it and millions of copies of the book are sold.

Being on the bestseller list, however, usually has more to do with subject matter than with talent; take away the content, which more often than not is beyond the writer's control in these cases, and you are left with very little. Any educated person could have written exactly the same book give or take a few words: there is no individual philosophical world-view, no contribution to literature as such.

This is why such writers are so often one-shot wonders: it is very rare for a person to experience an event of earth-shattering importance more than once or twice in a lifetime.

I believe it is very important to make a clear distinction between real literature that achieves mass appeal, like Balzac's work or that of Dickens, and those based solely on the value of the experience being recounted.

9 December 1999

The Arabic Novel

Some trace the origins of the Arabic novel back to the *Thousand and One Nights*, others to *Hadith Isa ibn Hisham*. Still others believe the novel is a foreign import from nineteenth-century Europe. My first concept of the novel was formed by the Qur'an. It attracted me as a fine form of the art of storytelling. Until today, the stories of the Qur'an have an unparalleled effect on the readers' feelings.

The stories told in the Qur'an follow the most modern principles of novel writing. They do not begin, like nineteenth-century novels, by setting the stage for the drama, then build up toward a climax, before reaching a resolution in the last pages. They are more like twentieth-century literary experiments, in which events do not follow a monotonous, diachronic sequence but move according to dramatic requirements, which dictate where the different parts of the story are located. In modern European novel writing, this represented a revolution, as can be seen in the works of Joyce or Proust.

In the Qur'an, the story of Mary, for example, is distributed among various *sura*s. Each of these contains part of the story. For this reason, the Qur'anic stories, with their noble content and style, were the first to provide me with a concept of the novel that I felt I could use in my own writing.

This effect extends throughout my work in general, but perhaps it is most apparent in *Morning and Evening Conversations*.

15 June 2000

Return of the Soul

I consider *Hadith Isa ibn Hisham* the first modern Egyptian novel. Although it has not received the attention it deserves from researchers, I believe it is a great work. It draws directly on the Arab heritage through its use of the *maqama* style. Its content of social criticism has shaped Egyptian novels until today. In fact, that novel affected our whole generation.

After *Isa ibn Hisham*, I read Muhammad Husayn Haykal, known as the father of the Egyptian novel, then Taha Husayn and al-Mazni. Then I reached Tawfiq al-Hakim, whose works were truly landmarks in the evolution of Arabic novel writing. In the truest sense, they represented and helped shape a new age.

Al-Hakim's writing ushered in a modern phase in the art of narration. In all truth, after the early sources of inspiration that shaped my concept of narration, such as the Qur'an, the *Thousand and One Nights*, and the epic tales that so fascinated me as a child, my direct mentor was al-Hakim. *The Return of the Soul* I believe marked the true birth of the Arabic novel. It was written using what were then cutting-edge narrative devices. Its predecessors, on the other hand, had turned toward the Western novels of the nineteenth century for inspiration. *The Return of the Soul*, in that context, was a bombshell.

29 June 2000

Young Writers

Young writers must study their craft closely. In order to do that, they must know their literature well. You may discover that some know of this or that foreign writer because they have heard his name mentioned on television, or been present at a discussion where his work was discussed; but if you ask them which of this writer's works they have read, they will grow embarrassed and fidget in their chairs, for they have never bothered to read one of his or her books. To write, the writer must learn from his predecessors' experience. If he does not, he will remain a prisoner of the confines of his own imagination.

Beyond literary culture, writers also need general culture. They must read history, politics, science, philosophy, psychology. They must study music and art. General knowledge is the raw material from which they will draw their inspiration, the petri dish in which their creativity can coalesce and bring forth a crystalized element of truth or beauty.

Then writers must strive not to let a day pass without at least making a stab at producing something new. Perhaps they will succeed, or maybe come up with a new idea that will blossom eventually. Perhaps they will complete a short story, and perhaps nothing will happen at all. At any rate, a writer must sit down to write every day, pick up his pen and try to write something—anything—on a piece of paper. Finally, writers must have endless patience. They must be always ready, for who knows when inspiration may strike?

14 September 2000

The Writer's Vision

The difference between a real writer and someone to whom writing is a mere hobby resides in the writer's vision. It is this vision, more than any other attribute, that defines a writer's approach: he wants to communicate all that he sees.

A vision is more general than either philosophy or ideology. Political opinion, for example, forms part of the writer's vision, but so do male–female relations and many other aspects of life. A vision encompasses and transcends all this.

The difference between Abu al-Alaa al-Ma'arri and Abu Nuwwas as two giants of Abbasid poetry can be described as the difference between pessimism and hedonism, in a nutshell. The vision develops as the author matures. In Abu Nuwwas, for example, profanity eventually gave way to wisdom and resignation, from pleasure to philosophical reflection.

As for my own vision, let my work speak for me on that front. All that matters is that what vision I have, I have endeavored to remain faithful to.

5 April 2001

Audience for Democracy

Democracy is the spirit of freedom. As such, it is not something to be granted by government alone, since unless it is deeply rooted, drawing nourishment from all sections of society, it is utterly worthless.

Today intellectuals and writers face an ever growing number of attacks, not from those in authority but from other groups so blinkered that they see only what they choose to see. It is a situation that contains many pitfalls for the creative artist and his endeavors.

Sometimes the writer is in an even more unfortunate position, caught in the crossfire between the authorities and groups hostile to such authority. The writer is sniped at from all directions.

Of course, the writer is never automatically in conflict with the ruling authority, nor is he by nature antagonistic to opposition factions. And in a true democracy all can cohabit.

Fortunately, the writer does have one recourse—he is protected by his public. Yet it is important to remember that it is democracy that accords such a large public to the writer. In earlier days culture was, after all, the prerogative of the elite, the monopoly of a ruling aristocracy. Kings and princes were both patrons and consumers; indeed, they were the only patrons and the only consumers. It is democracy that created a new audience for culture, an audience whose taste spans the most learned and the popular. Culture now belongs to all the people—it is this situation that has given the writer a potentially enormous audience and, with it, great influence.

30 November 1995

Pandora's Box

I have followed the debate concerning *For Bread Alone*, by Moroccan writer Mohamed Choukri, which was removed from the curriculum at the American University in Cairo, supposedly on account of the explicit sexual scenes it contains. I believe that a work of art must be evaluated according to artistic criteria alone, not according to moral or social principles. If a work of art appears to us as immoral, this is no doubt because of the seriousness and truthfulness that art demands, not because its author seeks to incite deviant behavior. Literature is literature, and nothing else.

This is why I disagree with Professor Galal Amin in his attack on *For Bread Alone*. He should have evaluated the book as Choukri's autobiography—in other words, in terms of its honesty and truthfulness. I admired Saad Zaghlul's honesty, for instance, when he admitted in his memoirs that he was an inveterate gambler. One can only be impressed by this nationalist icon's willingness to lay himself bare to scrutiny, and to hide nothing from himself or from others.

Such honesty in itself is eminently moral. Writers who admit to everything show courage, not depravity.

It is absolutely inadmissible that a book or a painting be banned because it is supposedly base. If we were to start condemning works on moral grounds, we would be unable to stop. We can, at most, give our opinion: it is not our right to prevent others from doing the same.

3 June 1999

Literature and Education

The inadequacy of education lies behind the current crisis in literature. Education shapes people, and it is shaping people who do not appreciate reading.

The educational system began to go wrong when the state realized that education was a right due to all the people. While this is certainly true, for it to make sense, the means to educate must be in place, means that include such things as teachers and classrooms. We were in a hurry, though, and instigated an educational system before we had the right instruments. As a result, classrooms became like overcrowded buses. There was standing room only.

Egyptian writers find themselves in crisis, facing a public that can rarely comprehend what they are writing. Literature has declined (here I speak qualitatively, not quantitatively) and is being replaced by lighter stuff.

There can be no doubt that a well-structured educational system could restore literature to its former status. The basis of any appreciation for literature is education and a concern for language. Once these two are in place, then literature would be in a position to regain its former centrality. But for this to happen there must be authors and readers. With these in place, the written word would be well able to withstand the competition constituted by television. Indeed, such competition could well constitute a stimulus rather than a challenge, to the production of serious literature.

23 March 1995

Serving Two Masters

It is difficult to combine two professions. I have never wanted to do anything more than write and have always been surprised at the ability of some people to continue writing while practicing professions far removed from the humanities. Nothing amazes me more than the doctor–poet.

Poetry is the result of sudden bursts of inspiration: a poet may receive the inspiration for a poem while sitting on a bus and be able to complete his poem as soon as he gets home. Novels and plays, on the other hand, are the results of many hours of work.

Ahmad Shawqi, sitting on the tram, would often be inspired to write, whereupon he would produce his packet of cigarettes and scribble lines on the back of the box so as not to forget them before he got home. Of course cigarette boxes really were boxes in those days, and so one could write a rather long poem on one.

Journalism is rather different, even though it may seem to be in direct contradiction with the arts and letters. Style and treatment are utterly different, but organization is all important. One must think only of structure. If a person can organize his time and thoughts, he can follow both professions, as did Ihsan Abd al-Quddus and Yusuf al-Siba'i.

5 October 1995

Attentive Readers

Literary writing is an art that focuses on the aesthetic above all else. Regardless of the social, political, or other subjects with which it deals, the content is always submerged within the formal qualities of the work. This is not the case with journalism, which is bound up with the description of events and the elucidation of social problems. Writing journalism requires a reasoned and consciously unsentimental approach to the material at hand.

A literary writer makes every effort to embellish and improve the word since such embellishment is part and parcel of the aesthetic of his working procedure. In a piece of journalism, though, such embellishment could well constitute an obstacle to direct communication with the targeted audience.

The best of today's journalists possess a lucid and simple style. In the past, though, it was the work of men of letters that you read on the pages of newspapers, not of professional journalists. In those days, of course, the job of the press was simple—to attack the occupation forces and sing the praise of the khedive. Given such an obvious mandate, literary writers could engage in rhetorical flourishes in their articles. Today's journalist is far different, say, from Mustafa al-Manfaluti, whose articles people would recite by heart. The readers, too, have changed from the time when, to my surprise, I once met an Iraqi in the Café Riche who could recite by heart the political articles of al-Aqqad.

22 August 1996

On Writing

Writing in my Mind

My recent work—the very short stories I now write, forced as I am by my infirmity to distill every phrase and every idea until I reach its very essence—has been compared more than once to haiku.

But Japanese poets are free to choose the terse yet eloquent form of this very stylized poetry.

As for me, necessity has compelled me to be brief; I can only write such short, condensed stories. I can no longer spend much time at my desk: half an hour a day, no more.

Of course, this does not suffice: I can spend many weeks on the same story, but ultimately its length will be determined by my exhaustion.

In truth, it would not be entirely fair to say that I work only half an hour a day, however: perhaps a single sentence will take half an hour for me to write, painstakingly, correcting a word here, revising a thought there.

But in reality I can spend days thinking about the story, mapping it out in my mind, until I can actually taste the words. I try out this sentence and that, this variation or that addition: I can see it all clearly. My mind bristles with the many possibilities open to me. Only when I have chosen the line the story will follow, when I have lined up the words in an order that suits me—only then do I take pen in hand for what I know will be a painful process.

2 January 1997

Story of a Notebook

It began a long time ago, this habit of keeping a notebook in which to jot down ideas as they came to me before they could be made into novels. It was a time of intellectual congestion, as it were. Ideas would begin to crowd into my head, and I was afraid that I might not find them once I started writing.

Still, the real drive behind writing, as I have always known, does not comprise ideas but something else. That happens or does not happen, regardless of whether or not there are ideas. And it comes with all that is necessary for creating a novel: characters, plots, ideas. Some call it inspiration of the muse: maybe it should be called lucidity.

I stopped writing for a few years after completing *The Cairo Trilogy;* I even thought I might never return to writing again. And at that time the notebook was, of course, of no use.

When I did return, finally, it was a different kind of writing altogether. What I had written in the notebook was utterly different in conception and tone, and it seemed pointless to resort to it again. The respected writer Abd al-Rahman al-Sharqawi did like one of the stories jotted down in the notebook—"al-Ataba al-Khadra," it was called—and spoke to me about turning it into a play. I gave my permission, but nothing came out of it in the end. And that, you could say, was the end of the notebook. A useless notebook, as it turns out.

11 January 2000

Customs of the Mind

My most important habit has been good organization, and I wouldn't have been able to achieve anything had I not set aside particular times for writing in the middle of all of life's preoccupations. I see writing as nine parts discipline and one part talent—the old inspiration and perspiration story. It was always very important for me to write every day—a question of not losing the habit.

For many years, there was my job as a civil servant, which occupied half the day, but the second half I spent reading and writing. It is necessary to spend some time every day immersed in one's craft. Reading words written by others is often just as important as writing itself. Then again, I also set aside time for friends—that is something to which I have always attached a great deal of importance. They took up the better part of the evening, after everyone was finished with their duties and responsibilities for the day.

I was not alone in being subject to that schedule, but what you could call my inspiration was strictly regimented too. Only at the time set aside for writing would I be ready to receive the tidings of my muse. Of course, in some cases I would sit for hours, pen in hand, sheet of paper on the table, and nothing would come to me. But in most cases I managed to fill the pages with writing.

No, I have never written anything in cafés, except for the details of some film scripts; all my literary works I composed during the hours of the day set aside for writing in my study.

20 July 2000

An Uninvited Courtship

I was deeply saddened when I learned from the media that certain people in Egypt were initiating court proceedings intending to divorce me from my wife, on the grounds that my novel, *Children of the Alley*, shows that I am an infidel. The raucous media circus appears to have been based on nothing more than the threat of such an action, which begs the question, how would the media react if such proceedings actually took place?

In some ways I should be glad to see *Children of the Alley* set before an honest judge. I know that the novel is not blasphemous and that I am no infidel. Indeed, when the novel was published thirty years ago I was told by Hasan Sabri al-Khuli, the then personal representative of President Gamal Abd al-Nasser, that a committee from al-Azhar would be coming to meet me to discuss the novel. I welcomed the meeting, and went to my office on the agreed date. No one came.

The only cause of distress about the whole business, apart from the negative light in which the foreign media will undoubtedly cast Egypt, is the fact that I might be forced to spend what few days are left to me in courthouses. I have never entered a courthouse in my life and now I feel a little too old to break the habits of a lifetime just to be dragged through the courts.

25 January 1996

Children of the Alley

In *Children of the Alley*, no one actually sees Gabalawi die, not even those who announce the news. Arafa, discovering that he has fallen under the dominance of the overseer after it is announced that Gabalawi is dead, responds by saying that Gabalawi must be brought back to life. What does this mean? In short, it implies that he is in need of a faith on which to base his knowledge, for the good of his district and people, and for their salvation.

Arafa discovers that all his learning is to no avail without the principles of Gabalawi. It is for this reason Arafa calls for the resurrection of Gabalawi—though of course Gabalawi had never died, nor was he resurrected. These are images, and they act on a symbolic level.

Ironically, the novel for which I was accused of blasphemy ends with the triumph of faith. Of course, Gabalawi is fiction. Like all art, it can be the vehicle for meanings that are the construction of the reader.

Yet *Children of the Alley* was intended as an Islamic novel. I refused to have it published in Egypt until it had the approval of al-Azhar, a refusal that is based on the fact that I am against neither religion nor al-Azhar.

1 June 1995

Slip of the Pen

One critic has remarked on the continuity and development of religious as opposed to socialist themes in my work. According to him, some critics in Egypt consider me a socialist but the truth of the matter, he says, is that I tend to sympathize with the thoughts of the Muslim Brotherhood. The evidence he adduces to this claim is that the communist character in *The Cairo Trilogy* had no children; the character who did have children was a Brotherhood member. This critic interpreted this as meaning that communist thought has no future in Egypt; the future belongs to the religious trends.

It has been half a century or so since I wrote the *Trilogy*. Since then, some say, communism has indeed died throughout the world, not only in Egypt. At the same time, we have witnessed the ascendance of religious thought, despite its extremist nature in some cases and its deviation from orthodox principles in others.

Yet I cannot say I was aware of this, or felt that it would happen, while writing the *Trilogy*. Part of the creative process is carried out by the unconscious mind, of course; the writer may not be aware of it at all. The critic did not necessarily find the material for his interpretation in black and white on the page; he read it into the story, and sought to analyze my character or convictions on that basis.

8 April 1999

Novel Inspiration

I have been asked, in the past, why I have produced only five short plays in my writing career as compared to fifty novels.

When inspiration comes to the writer it comes complete, as form and content, not as a vague idea to be put into verse or short story form. I am a novelist inasmuch as the ideas that come to me have tended, always, toward the form of a novel. Several of my short stories actually began life as parts of novels—retrieved from manuscripts that I had put to one side.

Strangely, a number of critics have been convinced that the process worked in reverse, and that I took short stories and expanded them into novels.

All of the five short plays I wrote after 1967. It was a time of great trauma, and in a way the plays are an extension of the kind of inner dialog that is such a strong feature of the kind of novel I wrote during the same period. At that time, I was thinking mostly in terms of dialog. It was, though, a period that came to an end, and I returned to the novel.

5 June 2001

The 1967 War

The date 5 June 1967 marked a major turning point in my writing. Take, for example, the theater of the absurd, which previously I used to read and enjoy, though I always felt it was alien to my writing. After 5 June, the absurd became the vision on which my novels were premised. I found myself writing in the absurd mode with the same spontaneity and dedication I had brought to my earlier realist novels. Hence such short stories as "Taht al-Mazalla" ('Under the Bus Shelter'), "Shahr al-Asal" ('Honeymoon'), and "Khammarat al-Qitt al-Aswad" ('The Black Cat Tavern').

For the first time, too, I found myself working in theater, writing five one-act plays. This is because dialog was in the grain of the moment—the dialog with reality in an attempt to come to grips with what had happened in the war and why it had happened. It was also dialog with the self, in search of the truth. And writing plays provided the ideal formulation for this dialog.

It can legitimately be argued that the quest for truth is the cardinal theme of everything I wrote after 5 June, be it fiction or drama. Throughout, I felt there was something missing, that what I was looking for did not even exist, that the question I was posing would remain unanswered—until that is, I became whole again and felt reborn with *The Harafish*, which I wrote after the October 1973 victory. For if 5 June 1967 was the worst day of my life, then 6 October 1973 was probably the happiest.

5 June 1997

Scholars and Cynics

After the Second World War many people in the West lost their faith and belief in God and embraced the absurd.

I too embraced some aspects of the absurd in my five one-act plays, and in some of my short stories. When the world around us loses its meaning, then the absurd seemed to represent the best way of expressing this concussion. However, my basic faith was firm and strong, and I was able to use the conventions of the absurd to portray a specific situation.

With regard to skepticism, I believe that it can take two directions—it can be a useful tool in the search for understanding, or it can become an end in itself. One school of thought is skeptical about everything, including belief in God and morality, while the other sees skepticism as the first step to true understanding. The latter, for instance, applied to Descartes, who decided that to understand the nature of being and to know the creator, he should start from point zero, rather than accept what others had said. From this point, Descartes arrived at a belief in God and nature and being. His was the skepticism of the scholar and not of the cynic.

25 May 1995

The Four Seasons

Some of my novels concern the seasons. For instance, *Autumn Quail* or *Love under the Rain* and other works where the main action takes place in summer or spring. Other works also included the winters and the summers, such as *The Cairo Trilogy* and *Miramar*, in which I described the Alexandrian winter at some length.

I remember in the English translation of *Miramar*, the writer of the preface remarked that he felt the rain was like the events of the novel, laying siege and pursuing the protagonists. In *Adrift on the Nile*, the events occurred over a whole year, including both winter and summer.

Winter is my favorite season, when I feel most strongly the urge to write. This has been the case ever since my childhood. When reading classical Arabic poetry, descriptions of winter would have much more effect on me than other verses.

Even though I do not write in summer, I would often walk along the banks of the Nile in Cairo or on the beach in Alexandria, and ideas would come to me that I would keep in mind and return to after the summer. I might sometimes make notes of these ideas, and sometimes merely memorize them until the time came for me to start writing again.

16 November 1995

Classical or Colloquial?

Islamic Arabic literature comprised the main component of my early education. I read the Qur'an and the *sunna* of the Prophet alongside such classics as *Kitab al-Aghani*. One title I well remember from those days is *Selected Arabic Literature*, a volume that began with selections of pre-Islamic poetry and ended with al-Manfaluti and al-Barudi. Such works deeply affected me and there can be no doubt that they had a profound influence on my literary style.

When I first began writing, it was in *fusha* (classical Arabic), even though the classical idiom was, at the time, coming under attack from many writers and intellectuals. Yet it was *fusha* that I choose when writing some of my most difficult, realist novels, a choice that forced many questions, not least how to convincingly give dialog to characters in alleyways. But the fact that many who read my novels are not consciously aware of whether my characters are speaking *fusha* or *amiyya* (colloquial Arabic) is, I like to think, proof that I overcame the problem.

I have always thought *fusha* particularly suitable for literature, and hope that my novels, greatly influenced by my reading of classical Arabic literature, have persuaded others of the validity of this view.

18 July 1996

The Sources

Besides the Qur'an, heroic epics formed my literary style. I remember reading *Antara Hamza al-Bahlawan* and other stories at an early age. Then I read the stories of the pre-Islamic Arabs and their wars. I was greatly affected by them. Then the *Thousand and One Nights*, with their unparalleled richness. Their density of detail and the sheer brilliance of the plot make them important narratives in human literature. Although their effect extended to European and other literature, their effect on us was greater because they emerged from this land and are infused with our Arab heritage.

Still, the *Thousand and One Nights* have a bad reputation. When we were young, we only read abridged versions—all the explicit scenes were censored. I later read the complete version. The tales express all the dreams that human beings share, yet some people have given themselves the right to confiscate parts of these dreams.

When Gabriel Garcia Marquez's novels were described in terms of magical realism, I immediately thought how appropriate that was to the *Thousand and One Nights*. That is where we must look to find the beginnings of magical realism. The stories combine reality and fantasy, truth and invention as no other narrative had done before. Perhaps none has been so successful since, either. And perhaps Latin American writers, among whom the school is so popular, were affected by the *Nights*, because the majority acknowledge the work's great artistic value.

22 June 2000

The Tree of Joy

The first time I heard of Taha Husayn, I was a student in secondary school. At the time he was already a legend: everyone was speaking of Taha Husayn because of the new ideas he was putting forth. His influence on me thus predated the impact of his writings, since I had already formed an impression of him before reading his books. I read his literary work before his political articles, in which he spoke out against the Wafd. I would read his newspaper column, *Wednesday Talks*, and I also read his *On the Margins of the Prophet's Biography* and *The Days*. This last book affected me especially.

Taha Husayn influenced my generation in two respects: first, through the intellectual revolution he brought about, and second, through *The Days*. Although this novel, as a literary framework, was marginal to his life, he presented in it several new forms for the writing of Arabic novels: he presented the autobiographical novel in *The Days*, just as he presented the romantic novel in *The Call of the Curlew*, and the novel as chronicle in *The Tree of Misery*. It was the first time I had read these kinds of novels; I was fascinated by Tolstoy and Thomas Mann. Perhaps I got the idea for my *Trilogy* while reading *The Tree of Misery*. I was bewitched by the idea of successive generations and the contradictions their lives could reveal, the history a family could tell, what they would feel.

12 November 1998

Bridge into France

Most of our writers were educated in the tradition of French literature and culture. Taha Husayn, Haykal, Tawfiq al-Hakim, Yahya Haqqi, and others were among this intellectual elite. But other prominent writers who never received a French education were equally fascinated with what French culture and literature had to offer. They read translations of novels by French writers, and thus transmitted to us new ideas and ways of writing.

Through such men as Abbas al-Aqqad, our knowledge of French culture and thought was enriched. Their work gave us an idea of French literature and allowed us to perceive life as presented in the world of *belles lettres*. These writers and translators were our bridge to another culture, a culture we could not have experienced otherwise because of the language barrier. These pioneers undertook the task of translating French works into Arabic, or simply writing about French culture.

Through their efforts Anatole France, André Gide, Malraux, and Guy de Maupassant became accessible to Arab readers. In fact, a school of short story writing established by Mahmud Taymur was influenced by Maupassant.

As for myself, I was deeply influenced by Flaubert, particularly *Madame Bovary*. I read most of Balzac in translation. But I read Zola's *Nana* in French. French literature has affected Arabic literature in diverse ways, which far exceed the influence of writings in other languages.

28 May 1998

Confessions

Self-disclosure is an important part of the Arabic literary tradition. The confessions of al-Ghazali are an important example, but not the only one. My fascination with Saad Zaghlul, the great nationalist leader, grew even deeper when I read his memoirs. A freedom fighter and icon of the Egyptian nationalist movement, he was not ashamed to lay bare his mistakes, detailing in black and white the sleepless nights spent in remorse and self-reproach.

Saad Zaghlul may have had a weakness for gambling, but he was distinguished by a rare moral courage. Only a few dare to expose their true selves, to put themselves on trial before their faceless, nameless readers, to ask themselves what their faults are, and what they have done to improve themselves. We all like to embellish our image, to seem perfect in the eyes of others, regardless of how distant we are from perfection.

I dealt with this duality in the character of Ahmad Abd al-Jawad in *The Cairo Trilogy*. The split in his personality allowed him to indulge his sensual nature while imposing strict asceticism on his family. While I saw this flaw as relatively harmless, I remember many men renowned for their patriotic rhetoric but who in truth were agents for the British.

23 July 1998

Friendly Pirates

My publisher, al-Sahhar, has over the years never dealt with me in anything but a correct and courteous way. However, no sooner is a book published in Egypt, or some work serialized in a newspaper or magazine, than one hears that it has been pirated and published in Lebanon or Morocco. This is not necessarily all bad since there is a large North African readership acquainted with my works largely through pirated editions.

Piracy, though it represents a financial loss, can also result in cultural gain. Often friends returning from abroad bring editions of my works that I did not know existed. I well remember receiving a letter from a reader informing me that one of my novels had been pirated and was selling in Lebanon, and that there were some differences with the version published by al-Sahhar.

Once I actually signed a contract with a copyright pirate. I was sitting in the Café Riche one day when a tall Lebanese man introduced himself to me saying: "I am the publisher who pirated all your novels from *The Mockery of the Fates* to *Miramar*." I asked him what he wanted and he explained that he wanted me to sign a contract entitling him to become my "official copyright pirate." Apparently, such was the competition between pirates that he wanted an exclusive deal. I was to receive my author's fees, of course. I found this extremely logical, and promptly signed the contract.

4 July 1996

Stories of Struggle

Someone told me recently that the Spanish newspaper *El Mundo* had chosen my novel *The Struggle for Thebes* as one of the most important novels of the twentieth century. I must say, I was amazed; at first, I thought they meant that it was the most important of my pharaonic novels, which I wrote before my realist phase. But then I learned that the newspaper had decided that *The Struggle for Thebes* incarnates the struggle of the Egyptian people against colonialism.

Such liberation movements may well have been the principal feature of the twentieth century, which witnessed the end of the great imperialist empires and the achievement of independence for indigenous peoples the world over. My novel linked the events taking place in Egypt at the time when I wrote it, under British occupation, with the historical dimension: events in the ancient Egyptian city of Thebes. So it was written in the spirit of national emancipation.

The Struggle for Thebes reflected the spirit of the age. I was glad to hear that it was received with great enthusiasm abroad when *El Mundo* decided to print it and distribute the novel with the newspaper.

But probably part of the interest is due to the global obsession with the pharaonic.

23 December 1999

Pulse of the Pen

A young man recently asked me: "How are you able to write of people's hope and pain, their joys and sorrows, in this way?" He added: "We see ourselves in everything you write, as if you were living the minute details of our daily life."

I have lived with people and shared their concerns. Every beat of society's pulse has resonated in my heart and overwhelmed me. Society, politics, daily life . . . I lived through every event with the people; their worries and aspirations were my own. Naturally, when I wrote, these feelings were reflected in my work. Must the writer belong, heart and soul, to a society? Yes, if he wishes his work to express something of that society.

Without even wanting or intending to, I found myself living people's problems. The problems were my daily life, and the beating of my heart. Without this experience, my work would have been entirely subjective, centered on my own feelings, desires, and dislikes. I would have been my own society.

I consider that what I have written has a lot to do with the people and not only with any gift or literary sensitivity I may have had. It is true that many people have gone through the same experiences as me, without necessarily writing about them in the same way or, for that matter, receiving a Nobel prize for their pains. But ultimately, one's way of writing comes down to what happens between the writer, the pen, and the paper, behind that locked door, in that empty room.

8 July 1999

A Variable Plunge

I have used all known methods of writing. Sometimes my stories were wholly or partly conceived when I started, and sometimes they had no shape in my mind at all.

Some stories I would enter into with prior awareness of all the dimensions that can be brought to bear on the telling of the tale in question: the events, the characters, down to the ending itself. In such cases, except for slight modifications inspired by the pen, the story does not alter during the process of writing.

But in other cases I would start without the slightest idea of what I was about to create. I would pick up the pen and write down a single sentence: *So-and-so walked into the alleyway*. And I would not know what So-and-so would be doing in that alleyway he had just entered; maybe I would not even know where that alleyway was. But a pertinent detail can bring forth all the details of the story before me. An evocative combination of letters is sometimes enough to summon an entire plot.

It is not necessary to be inspired or moved to write, in the usual sense. An experienced writer has a deep reserve of emotions, events, and characters on which he can always draw. Maybe, then, it is up to him to start anything at any time.

8 February 2001

Ancient Days

There are a number of reasons why my early works focused on ancient Egypt, though two stand out as being far more important than the others. Firstly, I would have to say, the 1919 Revolution had filled me with profound nationalist feelings, and this led, naturally, to a desire to probe into history in search of similar nationalist instances of rebellion against foreign occupation. Secondly, the discovery by Howard Carter of the tomb of Tutankhamun in 1922 created an unprecedented flurry of interest in ancient Egyptian history, not only in Egypt but all over the world.

Thus motivated, I read everything I could find, in Arabic, English, and French, about ancient Egypt. And as a result I could trace certain features of contemporary life to their origins thousands of years ago, often in very unexpected and at first glance far from obvious ways. I certainly reached the conclusion that the unity of the inhabitants of the Nile Valley, of which the 1919 Revolution was but one admittedly dramatic expression, was clearly rooted in the ancient history of the valley's inhabitants.

Since I had always nurtured the ambition to write novels set in ancient Egypt, I collected all the material I had found in history books and sifted through it for themes. Thus equipped, I wrote *The Mockery of the Fates*, followed by *Rhadopis*. With *The Struggle for Thebes*, I then lost interest in the ancient period, and became wholeheartedly focused on modern times. It was in an attempt to come to terms with a contemporary reality that I wrote *New Cairo*, and ever since that day I have been preoccupied, almost without exception, with the present.

In the seventies, however, I experienced a revival of interest in ancient Egyptian history, and began work on *Akhenaten: Dweller in Truth*, a novel that is the result of a new-found interest in the life and times of Akhenaten.

9 September 1999

Music Too

Music has been an inspiration to me for as long as I can remember. I knew the generation of musicians who first developed Arabic music along Turkish musical lines—Abduh al-Hamuli, Abd al-Hayy Hilmi, al-Manyalawi, and Saleh Abd al-Hayy. I knew, too, Sayyid Darwish, who raised Arabic music to new heights that were perfected by Muhammad Abd al-Wahab and Umm Kulthum.

I was also inspired by architecture, both ancient and Islamic, as representatives of two important strands of my national culture. In literature, I did not let myself be monopolized by our Arab heritage, but familiarized myself with foreign literature. I read English works in spite of my hatred for the British occupier. There were some who felt that English literature should be boycotted lest it should influence one to become pro-British, but I felt just the opposite. Literature—great, humane literature—always sides with liberty and equality.

There exist some very beautiful pharaonic passages, in both prose and verse, that I have repeatedly used in many of my works, including *The Mockery of the Fates*, *The Struggle for Thebes*, and *Akhenaten: Dweller in Truth.* They are motifs that also reappear in a great many of my short stories.

1 August 1996

Mother Egypt

Egyptian Identity

There has been much discussion concerning our identity. It is said that we are of pharaonic, not Arab, descent, that we are northerners and not Africans, or that we are Mediterranean peoples who have no roots in Asia.

In my opinion, our homeland is the source of our identity, something that has nothing to do with race. Egyptians represent an integral culture, formed by races of different civilizations—Arabs, Sudanese, Turks, and Moors, as well as ancient Egyptians. The common denominator has been our homeland, which has made one people of migrants of many races and civilizations, fusing their traits to form our national and cultural identity.

Once we were pharaonic. We became Greco-pharaonic, then Greco-Roman-pharaonic. Then we were Copts—at least until the Arabo-Islamic conquest. So how can we separate and distinguish all these cultural elements that have been molded together over the centuries to form a single nationality?

It is the homeland that bestows the feeling of identity. Our culture is of this land. We must not try to deconstruct this national character and reduce it to its original components, because that would cause it to lose all its cohesion. It would be like reducing water to oxygen and hydrogen—gases drifting away and disappearing in the air.

11 September 1997

Still flows the Nile

Raised in a poor district, far away from parks let alone water, my mother had a penchant, nonetheless, for nature, especially the river. It was a love of the Nile that she communicated to me. One of the most vivid memories I retain from childhood is standing on the Abu al-Ela Bridge and gazing down at the water, holding tightly onto my mother's hand.

The Nile has been a constant in my life. When I married, my wife and I moved into a houseboat, which is where I spent the happiest years of my life. I would open the windows every morning and instead of streets and traffic there was a vast expanse of shimmering water. On the opposite bank, beyond the water, I could see high trees and other houseboats, one owned by Ali Maher Pasha, the former prime minister, another by the singer Munira al-Mahdiya.

We left the houseboat and moved into an apartment that overlooked the Nile. During the long summer months, when I took a break from writing, I would sit for hours on the balcony staring at the sky and waiting for the moon to appear.

Old songs eulogized the Nile. In the past there was not one poet or singer who did not praise the river. Ahmad Shawqi, Hafez Ibrahim, Mahmud Hasan Ismail, Abd al-Wahab, and Umm Kulthum all acclaimed the Nile. Regrettably, the river now is all but invisible, shrouded by buildings and tea terraces that have been spawned along its banks. Behind them flows the same river our forefathers worshiped.

28 March 1996

Egyptian Calendar

Although I do not go out much, merely opening the window suffices to acquaint me with the weather. Many of my friends and acquaintances come to visit me and spend time recovering from their journey, no matter how short. They pant and mop their brows and drink glass after glass of cool water, complaining of the infernal heat.

Although the excessive heat and humidity are indeed unpleasant, there is nothing extraordinary about the weather. We are in the month of Ba'una, one of the hottest months of the year. Sometimes the weather does not correspond with the months of the Gregorian calendar that we now follow. This rarely happens, though, with our Coptic months. These are the old months that the Egyptians established by observing the succession of seasons and climatic changes over the years. They never fail.

The heritage of our ancestors is extremely important. Many of the elements present in our lives today originated with them. We are aware of only some, because our study of ancient Egypt has not yet solved all the puzzles of its civilization. The most important element of this heritage may be the deep religious belief that characterizes the Egyptian people. Ancient Egypt raised religion to a level unparalleled by any of the other ancient civilizations. Egypt, through Akhenaten, was the first civilization to call for monotheism.

6 July 2000

By the Sea

I first visited Alexandria, Egypt's second capital, in 1920, spending two weeks at San Stefano. How well I remember the beach there, divided into two sections, one for men and the other for women. Children would use the ladies' beach, where the slope was gentler and the water shallower. In those days, the entrance fee was two piasters, a sum that included the rental of a bathing suit together with, if needed, a gourd, which one would use much in the same way as an inflatable life belt, holding onto it to keep one's head above water. The sea by the men's beach was much rougher, and the waves would occasionally knock over the swimmers, my father included.

I remember returning home from my first trip to Alexandria dark as charcoal and so changed that at first my mother did not recognize me.

During my secondary school years, between 1925 and 1930 I went to Alexandria every year with my friends. My father would give me ten pounds, which covered all the expenses for food, lodging, and entertainment. My uncle, I remember, would become upset at such extravagance, and accuse my father of spoiling me, since ten pounds was far more than I would have earned had I been a graduate in his first job.

30 May 1996

One Egypt

The number of Catholics in this country is very small compared to the number of Orthodox Copts, but the visit of Pope John Paul II was not intended solely for the benefit of his Egyptian flock. Rather, it recognized Egypt's importance for the Christian community as a whole. It was here, after all, that the Holy Family sought refuge from Herod when he was massacring all the male children in Palestine. Jesus, Mary, and Joseph left Egypt only after Herod's death; had this country's people not offered them protection for three years, there would be no such thing as Christianity today. This is why the Pope described his visit as a pilgrimage, which he had been anticipating for long years.

John Paul II is the first Catholic pope to have made an official visit to Egypt. I only wish he had been able to stay longer, and visit more of the sites where the Holy Family stopped to rest. They are beautiful spots, which I know well; I visited them often as a boy. My mother took me to churches and monasteries as well as mosques and the shrines of revered Muslims.

One of the things that pleased me most about the Pope's visit was the great hospitality people showed him. Muslims attended the mass he gave, side by side with their Christian compatriots. My late friend Ibrahim Pasha Farag was always angry when people referred to Christians and Muslims in Egypt as forming two separate groups. "We are all one," he used to say. I was reminded of him when I saw my people come out to greet the Pope.

2 March 2000

Holy Family

The most important aspect of the current celebrations marking the two-thousandth anniversary of the Holy Family's flight into Egypt, in my opinion, is the fact that they serve to remind us of the strong link between Egypt and the prophets of monotheism. Egypt protected Christ when he was still a child, barely a few months old; he was brought here by his mother the Virgin Mary and Joseph the Carpenter as they obeyed the Lord and sought to escape Herod, who in his wrath had commanded that all male infants under the age of two be killed.

This is why Egypt and its people are blessed in the Bible. Indeed, the Bible contains many references to Egypt and the Egyptians as being blessed. The Qur'an, too, honors Mary, as it does no other woman in history.

The quality that makes Egypt unique in terms of religion is the country's special humanism. This is where Joseph came to work as overseer of Pharaoh's financial affairs; here, too, Moses grew up; if the Prophet Muhammad never saw this fair land, he married an Egyptian nonetheless.

This is why commemorating the flight of the Holy Family is so important, two thousand years after it took place. It reminds us once again of how special Egypt has been throughout its history.

1 June 2000

House of Books

Dar al-Kutub (the National Library), for so long a cornerstone on which the edifice of Egyptian culture has been built, is not an integral part of the new generation's cultural life because for many years it has been neglected, left to fall into a sad state of disrepair. Yet in my day it was the center of all intellectual endeavor—through preparatory and secondary school and into my college years, I would rely on the simple system of borrowing to read—on heritage, literature, art, history, politics, philosophy, and science. It was the reading of priceless literary classics that formed my concept of the novel.

A number of important authors worked there, including Hafiz Ibrahim and Tawfiq al-Hakim. To head the institution was regarded as the greatest honor. On a lighter note, it is worth adding that Ibrahim preferred having a humorous conference with one or more of his friends at the café opposite the Dar to sitting and reading inside it.

I was therefore greatly heartened to find out about plans to introduce an electronic classification system and develop the Dar once more—this, maybe, will be the beginning of the rebirth that is needed to bring the once central institution back into people's lives.

17 August 2000

Cross and Crescent

My generation was brought up in an atmosphere that was devoid of religious fanaticism. We were simply Egyptians, not Copts or Muslims.

I remember when the Egyptian cabinet consisted of only twelve ministers and when two of those were Copts. For many years, Wisa Wasef Pasha, a Copt, served as parliamentary speaker. Indeed, he became a national hero when he led the protest against the closing of parliament by the former prime minister Sidqi Pasha.

In those days Muslim candidates would stand in predominantly Coptic constituencies and vice versa. Ibrahim Pasha Farag once told me of an occasion when the Wafd party nominated a Copt in a Delta constituency. The candidate requested a transfer to a predominantly Coptic district, where he thought he would stand a better chance of winning. The leader of the Wafd at the time, Mustafa Pasha al-Nahas, told him that his nomination to a Muslim district was a deliberate choice. "Nurturing political awareness is more important than winning," he said. Interestingly enough, the candidate in question did win.

In my youth the first real intimation of the religion of neighbors from the district would often occur when someone had died and I found myself heading for a church to offer condolences. But even in death, Copts and Muslims observed very similar funeral rites. Some Copts held funeral processions while others erected pavilions to receive mourners.

Perhaps it is this atmosphere, which my generation imbibed,

that makes it particularly painful for us to witness the growth of religious fanaticism. For us it is an alien phenomenon, and any harm inflicted on our Coptic brothers is inflicted on us all.

21 March 1996

Metamorphosis

Islam is a religion that appeals to the intellect: it exalts knowledge, and accords scientists a preeminent place. It has drawn on some of the most humanistic elements of other civilizations, prohibiting discrimination on the basis of color or economic and social status. Absolute equality between rich and poor, rulers and subjects: this is the foundation of relations in an Islamic society.

In all philosophical and thought systems, however, there is a right and a left wing as well as the moderate center. The extremist exclusionary interpretation of Islam that prevails today is not a specificity of our times, nor an innovation. As everything depends on context, however, a phenomenon at which we used to laugh has become a very serious threat. When I was young, we found extremism laughable, because the social environment then was hostile to extremist ideas.

But the ideas we once mocked are gaining ground. Many Muslims continue to believe and practice their faith with the tolerance that used to be the norm. Yet there are others who, finding themselves in an altered environment, are fighting to survive. They have become fierce in their defense of their narrow interpretations. This poison has nothing to do with Islam, but it is no less deadly for all that.

23 April 1998

Religion and Violence

No religion condones violence; no religion condones terrorism. There has never been a religion that spread its beliefs by holding a knife to people's throats in order to force them to join the faith. And Islam, above all, is very clear that coercion of any kind has no place in religion. Whoever wishes to believe is free to do so; whoever does not so wish is equally free.

Of course, we can find examples in history of religion and violence being linked. But each example must be analyzed separately; every effect has its specific cause, and we should be cautious of generalization. The true example for us to hold in our minds in this and other regards is that of the Prophet and his Companions. The actions of the Mamluks and of the Turks cannot be held as authoritative: do we really want to take note of the example of the Umayyads or of the Khawarij over and above the rule of the Prophet and the caliph Omar ibn al-Khattab?

The answer is clearly no. The Khawarij, though extremely pious, provide the worst examples of religious extremism. It is recorded that they used to execute those accused of apostasy, for example. In my opinion, true religion, true Islam, is that of the Prophet Muhammad, who neither practiced nor believed in extremism. Nor did he sanction the execution of those accused of apostasy. Islam only resorted to violence in legitimate self-defense; any other form of violence betrays a lack of true understanding of the real nature of Islam, and is the responsibility wholly of those who practice it. It has no religious sanction.

Every creed or belief, unfortunately, attracts its share of

extremists. In the domain of ideas, different opinions are welcome, if these are expressed through civil dialog. Sadly, in a time of mounting social and economic problems, those with extremist ideas may find themselves resorting to crime and encouraging crime by others.

Terrorism must be confronted swiftly and severely. One can neither tolerate crime nor delay punishment. However, the issue of terrorism is not only a matter of state security. True, the state is doing its utmost to deal with this phenomenon as a matter of security. Yet the ideas behind terrorism remain in the air, and these should be met with other ideas.

5 January 1995

Days of Revolution

In my own works, politics are entwined in the lives and actions of my characters, as is religion, and perhaps—even—the spirit of humanity.

The reason for my concern with politics is simple. Each and every generation is political. In my case, and in the case of my generation, our early consciousness emerged and developed in the circumstances surrounding the popular national Egyptian revolution.

As a seven-year-old, I watched the developments of the revolution from behind my window. I witnessed revolution in the streets, flags flying high; I watched the battle with the British, heard the whistle of bullets, and saw the British cavalry slaughtering protestors. At that age I did not understand that I was living under occupation—I did not know the difference between living under occupation and being independent.

However, it was at this time that I began to ask questions and to understand the meaning of 'Englishman' and 'nationalist,' to understand the meaning of 'Saad Zaghlul' and 'exile.' I began to follow events. I began to pore over newspapers, and I cannot recall a single day when politics did not rear its head.

Yet I have never been a member of a political party. I have been unwilling to compromise myself to any single position. I have preferred to love freely and, it is true, hate freely. It is only when we come to count the cost of our love, and weigh it against gain and loss, that we become like politicians.

26 January 1995

Crisis Management

The Pakistani ambassador recently asked me how I thought the conflicts between Islam and modernity could be reconciled. I must confess that I find the terms of the question confusing, since the crisis between modernity and Islam seems to me little more than a fabrication.

The era of Muhammad Ali initiated a revival in every part of the nation's cultural and social life because Islam and modernity were reconciled. Our problem, then, lies not in creating the conditions necessary for Islam and modernity to coexist. Rather, we face a problem in reversing trends that have come recently to assume an importance they previously lacked. What is most necessary in Egypt is to halt the deterioration of our economy, the major cause of feelings of frustration and impotence. It is this frustration that has led sections of the population to search for alternatives in present-day fundamentalism.

There have always been those who claim that music is sinful, that every innovation is a deviation and every deviation leads to hell. But there is, in the end, very little that prevents somebody from performing their prayers in the morning and getting into their car in the afternoon. No one can tell you not to do this, just as no one in the West could tell you to change your religion.

The crisis of Islam and modernity—what to do? We must raise living standards and facilitate greater political participation, which means nurturing a greater democracy. We must allow anybody to form a political party. It is, after all, the people who must decide.

24 August 1995

The Body Politic

Fate and Destiny

"My Fate, My Destiny" is an old short story of mine. It is about a woman who gave birth to a child with two heads attached to one torso. She calls one head "My Fate," and the other "My Destiny." The story now seems to me strangely appropriate to Palestine, the land claimed by both Palestinians and Israelis. History has shown that separating the two is almost impossible. After endless wars and strife, the two parties have learned to accept one another, coexist, and share the same body.

In the story, My Fate takes the initiative toward peaceful coexistence, whereas My Destiny is more aggressive and less willing to coexist. The case is reminiscent of the situation in Palestine. The Israelis are much less determined than the Palestinians to live in peace and coexist on the same land.

The current Israeli government is trying to get all it can, and force the Palestinians to accept and submit to the status quo. But a peace built on submission is no lasting peace, only a brief cease-fire. History has taught us that things do not work in this manner. Humanity would have been saved the scourges of the Second World War had the Treaty of Versailles not forced Germany into complete submission. Such treaties are, in fact, the fuel of revolutions and rebellions, whereas our goal is to establish peace and coexistence.

Although in my story one of the twins dies, the other is told by doctors that he must carry his dead brother for the rest of his life. The two cannot be divided. Their coexistence is the only possible formula. They must cooperate and forget the past, as its woes are far outweighed by the innumerable benefits of the future if they manage to coexist in peace.

24 April 1997

Anwar al-Sadat

Anwar al-Sadat operated as a great statesman in the international arena.

He changed our image in the world. The painful memories of the June 1967 war, which so scarred the Egyptian consciousness and traumatized the Arabs, were wiped out by Anwar al-Sadat.

Like other leaders he had his weaknesses. In the opinion of some, his faults surpassed those of his predecessors, though perhaps we owe it to Sadat to forget all the mistakes of his presidency and instead remember him with gratitude, if only for the October victory, which raised Egypt and the whole Arab world, and marked the beginning of the long road to peace.

The only time I was prevented from writing occurred during Sadat's presidency, when, in early 1973, I signed a manifesto written by Tawfiq al-Hakim condemning the situation of no war, no peace. We were both barred from radio and television work, and it was prohibited to mention our names, even though we did not appear on the list of prohibited writers compiled by the State Information Organization.

Sadat's excuse for the ban was that, given preparations for the October War—of which we were unaware—he could ill afford internal opposition. I felt inspired by the October victory, by its spirit rather than by details of the operation. This, I think, is apparent in *The Harafish*, which was inspired by the events of 6 October. None of my previous works had been so full of optimism and of heroism.

2 March 1995

Cultural Manifestations

Every political system spawns its own culture. Democracies, though, have proved most able to sustain their cultures, to send out healthy sideshoots that flourish.

If they provide fertile ground for the growth of cultures, democracies also feed off their products. The relationship is symbiotic, which is not, necessarily, to imply that it is always easy. The relationship between political authority and culture has never been easy, whatever the political system. The political authority invariably craves or demands support, while the role of the intelligentsia is to act as the nation's conscience.

Cultural manifestations should, then, play an important role in drawing attention to the shortcomings of society, shortcomings in which the political authorities are invariably implicated. Yet the strength of democracy lies precisely in its ability to absorb such criticisms.

Dictators insist on their own dignity, a dignity to which it is easy to cause affront. In contrast, one might measure the strength of a democracy by the quantity of criticism that it is able to accept. Criticism becomes the daily bread on which any healthy democracy must feed.

When freedom of expression is guaranteed, culture, the arts, and intellectual life all flourish. Intellectuals are able to function to the best of their ability, and culture operates as a source of authority, coexisting with the political authority and informing its actions.

21 September 1995

Freedom of the Press

I support absolute and unconditional freedom of the press, for I believe it is the lung that allows the nation to breathe. This is especially true in this day and age: information has become the most powerful weapon in the world. He who knows wins. The press plays a crucial role in this respect.

The press, however, must also be responsible and honest. Those journalists who abuse freedom of expression to publish slander and calumny have no clue of the world we live in. President Mubarak has granted the press greater freedom than ever before—anyone who reads Egyptian newspapers, whether national or opposition, knows this.

There is a necessary and perpetual conflict between the press and the government: the newspapers want to publish everything, right now, while the government prefers to wait until political conditions are opportune. This conflict has raged all over the world, and continues to do so. Such a situation is normal, under any regime. When the conflict becomes an attempt to threaten and silence journalists by force, and inflict exaggerated punishments out of all proportion with crimes of publication, real or imagined, however—well, this is not the way press–government relations are managed in a democratic country. The conflict must never be allowed to escalate to such an extent that freedom of the press is stifled, especially in an era when censorship has become impossible.

11 November 1999

Abuses of Freedom

Abuses of press freedom are inevitable but better a thousand abuses and freedom than otherwise. Existing laws suffice to protect the reputation of individuals and protect the national interest. There is, too, a code of ethics by which writers and journalists must all abide.

I have myself been subjected to excessive criticism in the press. When this is purely literary, it is of little consequence. Political criticisms, though, have been painful. Whenever I make a political statement I have come to expect ten negative criticisms to each positive one. When, for instance, I call for peace and negotiations and am called an Israeli stooge I feel that I have faced an injustice, a feeling compounded by the fact that the people who make such accusations often come up to me and say that they knew that what they had written was untrue, but it was done to deter others.

And the remedy for this state of affairs lies not only with the law. We must accept some abuses if we also wish to be free. The counter to such abuses is to promote and refine our democratic processes. Abuses must be corrected through guidance, not by restricting freedom by passing legislation.

22 June 1995

True Heroism

Saad Zaghlul was a hero: anybody from my generation who was interested in politics began with Saad Zaghlul. He was a true patriot, and for many his career has come to mark the beginning of Egypt's recent history.

Unfortunately, I never met Zaghlul in the flesh. I thought once that I might meet the great man, when he was about to be received by the king at Abdin Palace. But I was mistaken: I went to the square, but there were thousands and thousands of people milling around in front of the palace. My ambition to see the great man was thwarted by the mass of people. So great were the crowds that I could not even see his car.

So I did not meet him, though he constituted the school from which everyone from my generation graduated. He was the person who taught us to love Egypt as much as we loved our own lives.

It is often suggested that after coming to power, Zaghlul's nationalism waned, and that his attitude toward the British softened to such an extent that he cooperated with them. This is not true. Zaghlul never changed his position toward the British. During his period in office, he achieved things that no other Egyptian ministry had been able to achieve, initiating reforms in the national interest. As for his relations with the British, after the assassination of the sirdar, the British forced Egypt out of Sudan. What could Zaghlul do against British force? When the opposition National Party criticized him he replied: "Give me the troops and I will confront the British."

When Allenby handed Zaghlul his famous ultimatum, breaking into the Council of Ministers with troops and cavalry, Zaghlul took the decree, read it, and said with a smile: "I was not aware that you had declared war."

I was greatly affected by Zaghlul's death. It would, I think, be no exaggeration to say that it was the one event that made the greatest impression on me, the single most important event of my life.

2 February 1995

The Eternal City

The EU's recent confirmation of its refusal to recognize Jerusalem as the unified capital of Israel simply ratified, in a sense, the conviction that prevails throughout the Arab world, and even, to a large extent, in the United States. A few years ago, when Congress suggested that the US Embassy in Israel be moved to Jerusalem from Tel Aviv, I remember that the White House expressed its reservations, and eventually the suggestion was shelved. This reflects the conscience of the world community, which cannot remain dormant forever.

Jerusalem, furthermore, is a special place, unlike any other city in the world. It cannot be dealt with as so much occupied or disputed territory. Perhaps this is why the 1947 Partition Plan stipulated its status as an international city, taking into account its exceptional sanctity. By occupying Arab Jerusalem, Israel professes that it has unified the city, although Israel should be the first to know the dangers of such a step—it was Hitler, after all, who sought to 'unify' Europe by occupying Germany's neighbors!

The Arabs do not oppose the unification of Jerusalem; they do oppose Israel's sole control over the city. Just as Israel would never relinquish Western Jerusalem, there is no reason that the Arabs should give up the Eastern sector. This is why the problem of Jerusalem should be solved in a radically different way.

18 March 1999

Triple Identity

All three great monotheistic religions teach their adherents that a part of Jerusalem belongs to them. This is a fact, and cannot be wished away.

As a consequence, the status of Jerusalem should be subject to negotiations. Can the Arabs really be asked to accept that Jerusalem become Israel's capital? Surely this would be a return to the situation that prevailed at the time of the Crusades, when the Christians tried to monopolize Jerusalem with the result that, for more than two centuries, liberating the city was the ambition of all Muslims.

Israel claims that it seeks to annex Jerusalem politically whilst allowing all religions access to their sacred places in the city. But when has politics ever left room for religion? When Israel recently barred Palestinians from the rest of Israel for political reasons, did it exempt those Palestinians who wanted to visit places of worship in Jerusalem, or pray at the Dome of the Rock, the focus of Muslim prayer before it was replaced by Mecca?

Peace could never be achieved, nor would basic intercourse be possible, as long as Jerusalem lay like a thorn in the hearts of Muslims. I am a believer in peace and as such I urge those responsible to ensure that Jerusalem, once a political settlement is achieved, becomes the subject of serious negotiations between the adherents of Judaism, Christianity, and Islam.

18 May 1995

Women's Liberation

Women's liberation movements are essential components of any renaissance in a people's history. A society cannot renew itself unless this is accompanied by a movement to liberate women.

In the early Islamic period, women were equal to men: they both stood side by side whether in poetry competitions or on the battlefield.

Our contemporary history offers many instances of women's liberation accompanying a general movement toward social regeneration. The 1919 Revolution infused Egyptian society with a progressive spirit that developed alongside powerful demands for the fulfillment of women's aspirations. This effervescence continued until the 1930s: among its supporters were Salama Musa, Taha Husayn, and the other literary figures of the enlightenment. During this period, Qasim Amin's books on women's liberation were reprinted. The same years saw Huda Sha'rawi's most intense activity, notably the establishment of the Egyptian Feminist Union.

The 1952 Revolution also gave women many social and political rights of which they had been deprived. This was the first time women were appointed to the posts of minister and ambassador.

Women's liberation is not limited to equal rights and duties: it also implies their full participation in the political and economic as well as social and cultural spheres. I remember women demonstrating in the 1930s, not only to demand their rights but essentially to call for an end to the British occupation. In the same way, we cannot exclude half of society from our shared development efforts. This is why I am a staunch supporter of the new National Women's Council, especially since its establishment comes at a time when half of society is being locked away from daily life.

16 March 2000

Not Anti-Arab

Somebody asked me the other day, "Why did you not image the Arab world in your novels?" I said, "I didn't even image the rest of Egypt itself in my work, and restricted myself to a small part of Cairo which became a backdrop to my works. My intention was not to image the whole of Egypt, much less the whole of the Arab world, because the writer chooses the setting of his narrative in accordance with artistic and dramatic necessities."

Whoever writes about me today, claiming that I am anti-Arab, relies on the fact that I am no longer able to read all I want to, because of the condition of my health and the weakness of my eyesight. But if you go back to the interview in question, you will realize that the headline says that I am against the Arabs, while the actual article does not say that. What can I do?

In fact, I do believe that all the Arab peoples are united in culture. There is also another unity that demands investigation: economic unity. Thirdly, there is the far-fetched goal of political unity. The cultural unity, a writer like myself cannot possibly overlook. The economic unity, I've constantly called for in my journalistic writings because economic collaboration and coordination imply more power for Arabs at large. And I believe that the realization of such unity (a common Arab market, for example) may well bring the desired political unity closer to realization. This is my opinion, but alas, many a young man has come to me for interviews and I welcome them, but no sooner do they go than I find such shocking headlines in the newspapers, completely unrelated to what I said.

3 August 2000

Gamal Abd al-Nasser

Gamal Abd al-Nasser was the leader of a revolution that radically changed the face of Egypt and the lives of Egyptians. The Revolution of 1952 revolutionized the social map of Egypt, raising the position of members of the popular classes several steps higher up on the social ladder and destroying feudalism without shedding a drop of blood. Nasser brought about reforms that Egypt had never before experienced. The only blemish on his record was his slide down the path of dictatorship (or maybe the slide of dictatorship down his path), as well as the maverick machinations of the intelligence agency and the secret police at the time. Quibbles about dictatorship apart, Nasser was one of the most exalted and respected leaders Egypt has ever had.

I came face to face with Nasser on several public occasions, such as when he bestowed on me the First Class Medal for Merit—the first state award I ever received. I was also awarded the State Merit Prize during Nasser's era, and any senior post I occupied or official function I performed belong also to that era.

My only personal encounter with him, however, came at the inauguration of *al-Ahram*'s new building in 1968. I was sitting with Husayn Fawzi, Salah Jahin, and Salah Taher when Nasser walked into the room with Muhammad Hasanayn Haykal, the paper's editor at the time, and said to Salah Jahin: "All the calf's-head meat you eat has made you very fat." He then turned to me and asked why I hadn't written any stories in *al-Ahram* for several weeks. Haykal replied that by coincidence once of my stories was appearing the following morning and that it was the kind of story that would get its writer into real trouble. Whereupon Nasser said to Haykal: "No, it may get you into trouble."

Indeed, Nasser was to the younger generations what Saad Zaghlul had been to people of my generation—a symbol of patriotism and a historic hero.

23 February 1995

Nasser's Death

In 1970, on the evening of 28 September, I returned with my wife and daughters from a month-long holiday in Alexandria. The house had been closed, there was nothing prepared for dinner, and so the servant was sent to get something from a nearby restaurant. He returned with incredible news. The president, he said, was dead. Turning on the television, I found that the servant was right. Gamal Abd al-Nasser had died and I found myself torn by conflicting emotions.

I disagreed, not with Nasser, but with his system of governing, and openly opposed him in several of my novels, particularly those written after the 1967 War. Abd al-Nasser accepted this opposition and never impounded my works, either in print or on film. Despite my objections to his rule, I would be among the first to acknowledge his tremendous achievements, not just in Egypt but throughout the Arab nation. And all I could think, on hearing the news of his death, was just how we might survive his absence.

Abd al-Nasser was dead, and we were without a leader who had had a profound influence on the whole world. We were without the man who had entered the heart of a nation in such a way that he had become an integral part of it. One could not conceive of life without him, and yet life without him was our only future.

At that moment I learned the true meaning of greatness and the true meaning of sorrow. That day I was more affected by conflicting emotions than ever before, or since.

28 September 1995

Power and Justice

The story of the attacks on the United States has a moral, but sadly nobody seems to be heeding it. The moral, or rather the most important of the many morals to be learned from these disastrous events, is that power alone is no guarantee of security. One may have the most highly developed, the most unprecedented weaponry in the history of humanity—nuclear, biological, chemical, and other arms that we have not yet heard of—and still one may receive a devastating blow. In the present case, as we have seen, all the terrorists needed were sharp blades; this fact alone demonstrates clearly how insufficient sheer military power is.

The only guarantee of security is justice. Had the United States been more just as the world's leader nobody would have plotted to destroy it.

The attacks mean only one thing: there are those in the world today who feel that US power is being used against them. America's power may indeed liquidate terrorist organizations and crush this or that dissident, but until the injustice ceases, violence and evil will not. The essence of ruling, as the old Arab adage maintains, is justice; the US needs to remove not only the evil perpetrators of such crimes but the causes of injustice in the world.

27 September 2001

The World
of Tomorrow

Ready for It

We continue to speak of the twenty-first century as a far-off land, which we must traverse eons to reach—yet it is upon us. In a matter of days, the new century will begin. What have we done to prepare ourselves? Some see the new era simply as a continuation of the old: just as we pass from December to January, so will we slip across the threshold of this new beginning. The truth, however, is that things are not so simple. Great changes are taking place before our eyes, and will be revealed suddenly, when it is already too late to follow the metamorphosis. The science-fiction future is reality; moreover, it is only days away.

The old political configuration is no more; the monolith of unprecedented American supremacy has replaced the blocs of battling nation-states. Although the status of the United States as a global superpower has been a reality since the end of the Second World War, there is a fundamental difference between a great power whose sway is offset by the presence of another, and one that dominates in the absence of all rivals. This new situation will shape the political landscape in the coming century. The expansion of the market economy will also impose new relations both within and among the members of the international community; then there is the impact on culture of information technology, and the fact that communications now render borders redundant. These, then, are the features of the new century. Are we ready?

16 December 1999

Millennial Faith

Will the twenty-first century be marked by more world wars like those that wreaked devastation on an unprecedented scale during our time? I do not think so; indeed, I very much doubt that wars of that sort, in which two global superpowers confront each other, will have any place in the new millennium. What we will see, instead, are many regional wars, fought over religion or ethnicity.

André Malraux once said that the next century would be a religious century, or would not be at all. Well, I believe that three great values mark an individual's life: truth, good, and beauty. During the twentieth century, we have discovered that science, in searching for truth, eliminated good, while art, in striving for beauty, has eliminated ethics. In this perspective, in fact, the revival of religious conflict may be seen as an attempt to recover a moral code that has been absent from our lives during the better part of this century.

Perhaps this is what Malraux had in mind when he spoke of the preponderance of religion in the coming century. Still, I disagree with him: there are many things in a human being's life that will enter into competition with religious conviction; whether or not this will be to our benefit remains to be seen.

22 April 1999

Conflict or Debate?

The next international conflict will not be between nations but between cultures. Rivalry and opposition, divergence and convergence have always existed among the cultures of the world, in unipolar or multipolar systems. We must endeavor to prevent the relation between cultures from developing into conflict. We need a dialog, because the world is now smaller than it ever was. For example, the internet has opened windows all over the world. It is natural that different cultures and civilizations will acquire greater influence, and this will help dialog to develop.

So why should we assume confrontation? True, there will always be rivalry between cultures, but this is a welcome phenomenon, since it will favor the fitter and more efficient rather than the more powerful. No matter how powerful a culture may be militarily or politically, it cannot impose itself upon a people unless they are convinced of its superiority to their own culture. If they are convinced, then the new culture is more qualified than the one it replaced.

There is no hatred involved in cultural rivalry, nor should it ever reach the point of confrontation. Were it to reach that point, it would be a sign that we are witnessing not a cultural conflict but a political battle—a very different issue. Cultures should engage only in dialog. Either one culture will emerge as the most appropriate, or various cultures will coexist. There is always room for a plurality of cultures in art, ideas, and literature.

8 May 1997

Getting it Right

The Universal Declaration of Human Rights is among humanity's greatest achievements in the twentieth century. Tragically, however, these rights are being trampled underfoot today: men and women everywhere are forced to demand their fundamental freedoms, yet their cries often fall on deaf ears. Still, before the declaration was ratified, even such demands could not be contemplated. The violation of what we consider today basic rights of all human beings was routine—the natural order of things.

The declaration created awareness that humanity shared certain basic and inalienable rights. US president Woodrow Wilson's principles, declared as the First World War was coming to an end, were the basis of all the revolutions of subsequent years. They crystalized a new awareness that the 'natural order' was not so natural after all. Sometimes awareness is the most important factor in achieving a desired goal.

We live today in unprecedented circumstances, for awareness of human rights is almost universal. Even leaders who do not guarantee their citizen's human rights pay lip service to the idea, by recognizing the importance of such rights, at least in theory. In countries where human rights are violated, efforts are made to mask violations. The rights of women, children, minorities—even animals—are demanded or defended worldwide. I believe the twenty-first century will be known as the century of human rights.

13 January 2000

Space and Beyond

Until the twentieth century, human beings regarded outer space as fish do dry land: as the great beyond, the boundary beyond which life was impossible. Perhaps the conquest of space, then, is the true turning point at which it became possible to contemplate extending our natural habitat beyond the Earth's atmosphere. Satellites now revolve quite quietly in space; human beings can travel beyond limits that were virtually unimaginable before 1900. This conquest is as yet incomplete, of course; what we are experiencing now is only the beginning, and I believe that, in this new century, the other planets of our galaxy will become so many new worlds for humanity to explore.

In politics, one of the last century's greatest human achievements was the liberation of the peoples of the Third World from imperialism, which in some areas was several centuries old. The uprisings that shook the world, especially at mid-century, were unprecedented; they redrew the old maps, creating new countries and dividing or erasing old ones; most importantly, these great liberation movements also redressed the political balance of power, by giving voice to millions who had been silenced throughout history. At the end of the twentieth century, these aspirations were transmitted from Asia, Africa, and Latin America to Eastern Europe, to Yugoslavia and Czechoslovakia and the GDR. They transported us forward into a new era, one of radically different political realities.

6 January 2000

Cloning, Not Creation

I am against those who wish to ban cloning, for knowledge should never be treated in that manner. We must not be afraid of negative fallout from a discovery; in fact, our duty is to give scientists complete freedom of action in experimentation and discovery. This should not worry us; if experiments are permissible with the plants created by God, then why should they not be permissible with animals and humans? The result need not be limited to the duplication of a human; in theory, a clone could be free of the subject's faults and blemishes, which is a genetic advance not to be ignored, and is neither blasphemous nor irreverent.

To those who claim that creation is an attribute of God and God alone, I reply: justice, mercy, and generosity are also attributes of God. Should that stop people from being just, merciful, or generous? These attributes in God are one thing, in man another.

Besides, there is absolutely no creation concerned in cloning, since it is merely a matter of fertilizing an ovum that already has specific characteristics. The ovum is then placed in the uterus of a woman and becomes an embryo in the normal manner. The whole operation, then, is close to artificial insemination (which is practiced worldwide and is not at all an attempt at creation)—but may also be an attempt to control the genetic attributes of embryos to produce improved progeny—in the same manner as standard cross-breeding, but in an improved form.

I fail to see how this could constitute a transgression of religion: God created humans with the divine knowledge that the boundaries of their discoveries could encompass cloning; the scientist involved in cloning was himself made by God, who is aware that His creations are capable of scientific creativity.

3 April 1997

Not Just Cellular

Cloning is neither good nor bad: it is a new scientific experiment, and one must not stand in the way of scientific research. History bears testimony to this imperative: every time mankind attempted to block scientific progress it proved a mistake, from Galileo to the present.

Fear of progress is a moral not a scientific consideration. The annihilation of the population of Nagasaki and Hiroshima was a moral issue, unrelated to the scientific nature of the atom. The atom is invaluable in science, in medicine, and in agriculture; progress must not be hindered just because humans are morally deviant. It is up to us to instruct mankind.

Cloning is not simply a matter of cells. If one were to clone an individual from Hitler's cells, that would not necessarily result in a repetition of World War Two. The environment clearly plays a role. If a Hitler was created today in Germany, with all Hitler's characteristics, he might become an artist and depict the world of his dreams; instead of destroying the world, he might destroy realism. Human beings are conditioned by their environment, not just by their DNA. Hitler's choices were not only the result of innate characteristics, but were also conditioned by the Versailles Treaty and a humiliated Germany that was bound to rise and rebel.

It is said that tampering with genetics is against the divine laws ordained by God. Taking an artery from a man's leg and inserting it into his heart is also against divine injunctions, as is the implantation of an animal's liver into a human body. So, too, is exploring the depths of the oceans.

God gave man a brain and empowered him to achieve all these things as a service to humanity and progress, so we must not refuse the challenge.

10 April 1997

Choosing Armageddon

I paused recently at an item I read in the paper, and paused again when I realized I had been thinking about it almost every day. In fact, I still can't bring myself to forget it.

The news concerned perdition: the world, I realized, had already been demolished twice, completely eliminated. This was the strangest part: people assume that when the world is thus abolished, there will be nothing left. Yet, as I was finding out for the first time, the world had already disappeared not once but twice. And on each occasion every form of living being—every sign of life on earth, in fact, completely vanished.

If it has happened twice, it might happen a third time, any minute now: a stray asteroid or some other astral body could hit the earth and that would be the end of everything. Perhaps modern science allows us to account for and predict phenomena to some degree, so we may have a general idea of when this will happen, but even then we still cannot possibly prevent it.

Whereas before the danger came only from natural phenomena, now we have weapons of mass destruction and environmental hazards too. When it comes to perdition of the third degree—and this is the most disturbing thought—the end of the world will be the prerogative of humanity.

29 January 1998

Clean Africa

I was delighted by the recent Cairo announcement declaring Africa a nuclear-free area. I have opposed nuclear weapons for as long as I remember, not least for the simple reason that they harm the possessor as much as they harm anyone. They constitute the most desperate instruments of revenge, capable of destroying everything. Nuclear weapons are the only weapons that affect the entire population of the globe—simply remember Chernobyl, a limited disaster that occurred more than a decade ago, but which continues to affect people thousands of miles away from the former Soviet Union.

There can be no absolute guarantee that nuclear weapons will not be used in a moment of anger or of desperation. There can be no guarantee that nuclear weapons will be kept out of the hands of the unscrupulous, the irresponsible, or those whose stock in trade is terror. Though there is no limit to the horrors the use of such weapons can bring, neither can we guarantee that people will be cowed by this fact. There are, and always will be, those who care nothing about the consequences of their actions.

We face a very simple fact. We can never be entirely sure that weapons of mass destruction will not fall into the hands of the irresponsible, the nightmare scenario being, of course, that a terrorist group obtains a nuclear weapon and threatens to use it, or worse still, actually does. The only absolute guarantee of avoiding such a scenario is to abandon nuclear weapons all together.

Nuclear weapons should gradually be discarded until the world

is completely free of their evil. What pleases me about the Cairo declaration is that our continent should have taken the first step and declared itself nuclear-free. How I wish that our neighbors would follow suit.

18 April 1996

Weapons of Reason

How can Third World governments that censor the media stop something from appearing in the press if the public can see it on television via satellite dishes, or if people can download it through the internet?

If everything becomes possible and permissible, we are bound to clash with many things that go against our traditions, customs, and culture. What must we do?

In my opinion, the solution lies in the strengthening of our cultural heritage. We must increase its immune system so that it can withstand the cultural invasion sweeping over us like a tidal wave. Only an educational revolution adapted to the modern age of information can achieve this goal.

Thinking or exercising the brain is what distinguishes human beings from other creatures. But some educational systems in developing countries are not designed with a view to teaching students how to think, how to reach conclusions that may differ from the textbook. Creative thinking is encouraged and rewarded abroad, whereas here any departure from the textbook is punished. A student who dares to express an original idea will be immediately failed for not repeating what he has been taught.

But if we can succeed in properly educating young people we need not worry about what they hear or see. They will be protected by the most powerful weapon in the world—the rational mind.

26 September 1996

On Ethics

I firmly believe that ethics, at both the individual and societal levels, are of the greatest importance, since morals are the basis of good faith and successful social intercourse. Those living in a society which cares for ethical values such as generosity, a sense of honor, and truthfulness, feel secure and safe. But if one finds oneself among people who do not consider ethical conduct important, one has no confidence in anyone, and feels unable to have any dealing without witnesses and documents, because nobody is to be trusted.

No society can exist without an ethical base. When contaminated food is unloaded onto the market, or when buildings collapse, we have proof of deteriorating moral values in society. We may think transactions are based on laws and regulations, but these are merely devices for putting ethics into legal terminology. In the last analysis, transactions are based on ethics.

People in many eras have looked back with nostalgia to a more moral past. It is natural for people to feel this way, but it is in fact more a reflection of the difficulties they have in dealing with their present reality than a realistic indication of society's decline. It is interesting to note that some ancient Egyptian papyri were found to contain personal letters in which the writer complained about the deteriorating morality in his era, compared to that of previous generations. After all, the past is the recollections of our forebears, and we tend not to remember the pettiness, the dishonest transactions, but recall only the good and the wonderful things that will not be a burden to us.

We must not, however, forget the economic factor. In

moments of economic crisis the pressure on morality is much greater than in times of plenty. Dire economic straits are a great test of morality, and man is, after all like a day—half is in daylight and half is kept in the dark. People generally show one side and hide the other. When circumstances change, the other side appears.

14 November 1996

Life's Meaning

Bearing in mind all that humanity has acquired through technological progress, what role now remains for religion?

Religion is still essential nowadays, even after all the scientific progress that mankind has made. Indeed, man's new-found power necessitates a greater regard for humanitarian principles and ethical conduct, since if this were not the case, there would be a danger of man being directed by self-interest and narrowly conceived reason alone. We have all seen where such a materialistic path can lead.

The crime and violence that we see all around us today is the result of the disassociation of human reason and human self-interest from the guiding path of principle. When man abides by the precepts of religion, however, the awareness of such a path is innate within him.

It is true that many modern philosophies have tried to replace God with non-religiously derived ethical systems. Jean-Jacques Rousseau's ideas are not so very far from Christianity, and nor are those of Francis Bacon. But a solely human search for truth and for right conduct is not the same as the guidance given by faith, since faith is given by God, and this is the essential difference between the two.

Therefore, however excellent humanistic ethics may be, only those who truly have faith are prepared to die in the cause of some higher principle or ethical system. Faith is always behind self-sacrifice, as a purely individual and rational persuasion cannot be, and this is why we are in need of religion for religion's sake alone.

Those who appeal solely to human reason in their search for guidance will still have doubts, will still ask what holds them to follow their own ethical precepts. Why should certain things be given up, after all, if they are to be replaced only with a few rational precepts?

But when these precepts are given by God Almighty, then they have a wholly different meaning and moral force. God alone gives value and gives value to existence. Without Him, life has no meaning, values have no meaning, and all effort is futile.

29 December 1994

Glossary

5 June 1967: defeat of Egypt and Israel's occupation of Sinai.

6 October 1973: Egyptian victory in breaking through Israel's defenses to cross the Suez Canal and reenter Sinai.

1919 Revolution: popular uprising against the British occupation.

1952 Revolution: coup on 23 July in which Gamal Abd al-Nasser and the Free Officers overthrew King Farouk.

Abaza, Tharwat: renowned Egyptian novelist, 1927–.

Abbasid: the Iraqi dynasty that ruled Egypt from 750 to 969.

al-Abbasiya: suburb northeast of central Cairo, newly built in the desert at the time Mahfouz's family moved there.

Abd al-Hayy, Saleh: popular Egyptian singer in the 1930s and 1940s, 1896–1962.

Abd al-Nasser, Gamal: leader of the Free Officers' coup of July 1952; president of the republic from 1954 until his death in 1970.

Abd al-Quddus, Ihsan: journalist, novelist, and playwright, 1919–90.

Abd al-Wahab, Muhammad: actor, singer, and composer, 1900–91.

Abu al-Alaa al-Ma'arri: Ahmad ibn Abdallah ibn Sulayman, blind poet, 974–1057.

Abu Nuwwas: classical Arab poet, 756?–814.

Abu Seif, Salah: film director, 1915–96.

Afifi, Muhammad: Egyptian satirist of the mid-twentieth century.

al-Ahram: Egypt's leading daily newspaper, founded in 1876.

Allenby, Edmund Henry, Viscount: English military leader and colonial administrator, 1861–1936.

Amin, Ahmad: Arabic scholar, teacher, and editor, 1886–1954.

Amin, Qasim: lawyer and author of *The Liberation of Women* (1899), 1863–1908.

al-Aqqad, Abbas: journalist, poet, and writer, 1889–1964.

Ashura: the anniversary of the martyrdom of Husayn, grandson of the Prophet Muhammad.

al-Ataba al-Khadra: commercial area of Cairo between the old Islamic city and downtown.

Awad, Louis: essayist and literary critic, 1914–90.

Azbakiya Gardens: pleasure gardens adjoining downtown Cairo.

Baha al-Din, Ahmad: journalist, author, and editor, 1927–96.

Bakathir, Ali Ahmad: playwright, 1910–69.

al-Barudi, Mahmud Sami: army officer, prime minister, and poet, 1839–1904.

Café Riche: café, restaurant, and bar in downtown Cairo popular with artists, writers, and intellectuals.

Choukri, Mohamed: contemporary Moroccan novelist.

Copt: an Egyptian Orthodox Christian.

couscous: North African dish, savory or sweet, made from semolina.

Darwish, Sayyid: Alexandrian composer and singer, 1892–1923.

Eid: see 'feast.'

Farag, Ibrahim Pasha: lawyer, prominent Wafdist leader, 1903–94.

Farid, Muhammad: nationalist leader, writer, and lawyer, 1868–1919.

fatta: dish eaten especially at the Great Feast, made from bread and rice soaked in a garlic-rich meat stock.

Fawzi, Husayn: artist, musician, and writer, 1900–88.

feast (Eid): either the 'Great Feast,' which commemorates Abraham's sacrifice of the lamb in place of his son, or the 'Small Feast,' which ends the fasting month of Ramadan.

***futuwwa* (pl. *futuwwat*)**: neighborhood tough, both protector and bully.

fuul: staple Egyptian dish of stewed beans, usually served with oil and seasoning.

al-Gamaliya: area within the medieval heart of Cairo, between the Husayn Mosque and the North Walls.

Glymenopoulos: a beach suburb of Alexandria, often abbreviated to 'Gleem.'

Hadith Isa ibn Hisham: early Arabic novel by Muhammad al-Muwaylhi, 1858–1930.

hadith: sayings of the Prophet Muhammad.

al-Hakim, Tawfiq: playwright, novelist, and essayist, 1898–1987.

al-Hamuli, Abduh: musician, singer, and composer, 1840?–1901.

Haqqi, Yahya: novelist, short-story writer, and critic, 1905–92.

Harafish: 'Riffraff,' the name by which Mahfouz's circle of friends was known; his novel *The Harafish* took its name from them.

Haykal, Muhammad Hasanayn: political journalist, writer, and editor, 1923–.

Haykal, Muhammad Husayn: writer, politician, and lawyer, 1888–1956.

al-Husayn: district of Islamic Cairo around the Husayn Mosque.

Husayn, Taha: writer, educational administrator, and minister, 1889–1973.

Ibrahim, Hafez: nationalist poet, 1871–1932.

Ismail, Mahmud Hasan: Egyptian poet, 1910–77.

Jahin, Salah: cartoonist, poet, playwright, and actor, 1930–1986.

kahk: a kind of shortbread baked for the Small Feast.

Kamel, Fuad: twentieth-century Egyptian abstract painter.

Kamel, Mustafa: nationalist leader, orator, and editor, 1874–1908.

Khawarij: dissenting sect of early Islam.

khedive: title of rulers of Egypt from 1867 to 1914.

Kitab al-Aghani: written by Abu al-Farag al-Isfahani, b. 897.

LE: see 'pound.'

ma'allim: title of respect in traditional society for a foreman, shopkeeper, or gang leader.

al-Mahdiya, Munira: actress and singer, 1884–1965.

Maher Pasha, Ali: four times prime minister of Egypt, 1882–1960.

Mahmud, Mustafa: physician, journalist, and writer, 1921–.

al-Manfaluti, Mustafa: writer and poet, 1876–1924.

***maqama* style**: a genre of Arabic rhythmic prose.

Mazhar, Ahmad: actor and equestrian, member of the Harafish, 1917–.

al-Mazni, Abd al-Qader: writer, journalist, and poet, 1889–1949.

Mubarak, Husni: pilot and president of Egypt, 1928–.

mulid: annual celebration in memory of a revered religious figure.

Mulid al-Nabi: *mulid* of the Prophet Muhammad.

Musa, Salama: journalist and writer, 1887–1958.

al-Nahas Pasha, Mustafa: Wafd party leader and five times prime minister of Egypt, 1879–1965.

Omar ibn al-Khattab: the second caliph (successor of the Prophet Muhammad).

piaster: see 'pound.'

pound: 100 piasters make one Egyptian pound (LE), which at 2001 rates is approximately equivalent to $0.25.

Qut al-Qulub al-Dimardashiya: Egyptian author of a number of novels in French, 1892–1968.

Ramadan: holy month in the Islamic calendar, marked by daytime fasting.

al-Sadat, Anwar: Free Officer and president of Egypt, 1918–81.

Said, Mahmud: artist and lawyer, 1897–1964.

Sha'rawi, Huda: pioneer feminist leader, 1879–1947.

Shawqi, Ahmad: poet and playwright, 1868–1932.

shisha: waterpipe for smoking honeyed tobacco.

al-Siba'i, Yusuf: journalist, and writer, 1917–78.

Sidqi Pasha, Ismail: minister and prime minister, 1875–1948.

sirdar: title of the British commander of the Egyptian army.

sunna: the traditions of the life of the Prophet Muhammad.

sura: a verse of the Qur'an.

Taher, Salah: Egyptian artist, 1911–.

Taymur, Mahmud: writer of novels, short stories, and plays, 1894–1973.

Umayyads: Arab dynasty that ruled Egypt from 661 to 750.

Umm Kulthum: the most popular female singer in the Arab world, 1904?–1975.

Wafd: political party opposed to the British occupation of Egypt.

Wasef Pasha, Wisa: speaker of the Egyptian parliament, 1873–1946.

Wayli police station: the main police station in Abbasiya.

Yunan, Ramses: Egyptian surrealist painter, 1913–66.

Zaghlul, Saad: lawyer, minister, leader of the Wafd, prime minister, and nationalist hero, 1859–1927.

al-Zayyat, Ahmad Hasan: Arabic scholar and writer, 1885–1968.